Perspectives *on* Behaviour

Perspectives *on* Behaviour

A Practical Guide to Effective Interventions for Teachers

Second Edition

Harry Ayers, Don Clarke and Anne Murray

David Fulton Publishers
London

David Fulton Publishers Ltd
Ormond House, 26–27 Boswell Street, London WC1N 3JD

First published in Great Britain by David Fulton Publishers 1995
Reprinted 1996, 1997 and 1998

Second edition published 2000

Note: The right of Harry Ayers, Don Clarke and Anne Murray to be identified as the authors of this work has been asserted by them in accordance with the Copyright, Designs and Patents Act 1988.

Copyright © The London Borough of Tower Hamlets; Support for Learning 2000

British Library Cataloguing in Publication Data

A catalogue record for this book is available from the British Library

ISBN 1–85346–672–7

Typeset by FSH Ltd, London
Printed in Great Britain by Bell and Bain Ltd, Glasgow

Contents

Preface

General issues and controversies surrounding behaviour

Differences in terminology used to describe behaviour and behavioural problems

Different terms are used to describe behaviour, e.g. in child psychiatry reference is made to mental disorders such as anxiety disorder, autism and ADHD; in the SEN Code of Practice the terms emotional and behavioural difficulties are used and also in current usage the terms internalising and externalising disorder are employed. The categorisation of behaviour into types and subtypes has proliferated along with the question of whether a particular problem is being over- or under-diagnosed. Teachers should be clear that they are using terms according to their correct definitions or what they mean by the use of particular terms. Specific, descriptive phrases should be used instead of vague colloquialisms.

Assessment and classification of behaviour

Questions regarding the validity and reliability of classification systems are sometimes raised, e.g. with regard to DSM IV and ICD 10. The term diagnosis is used analogously with medical evaluation and decisions are made according to whether a person's pattern of symptoms meets certain criteria for a term or category to be applied. Categories are seen by some as depending on arbitrary cut-off points. Some think that behaviour is best described in dimensional rather than categorical terms, i.e. all behaviour lies along a dimension, a difference in degree rather than kind. Teachers should be aware that behavioural differences may not be clear-cut and that there may be overlaps between different behaviours. Some problems may occur along with others; where this happens it is called co-morbidity. Furthermore, it is important to note that behavioural descriptions or terms do not constitute explanations and the application of such terms can have a stigmatising effect. It is also the case that assessment can be influenced by the behaviour of the assessor, the attributes of the assessor, the model of assessment used, bias and by a tendency for assessors to concentrate on weaknesses rather than strengths. Finally an assessment may not be properly conducted and may be overly influenced by the person or institution for whom it is being undertaken.

Causation and methodology in relation to behaviour

Different perspectives subscribe to different causal models, e.g. the behavioural approach is based on classical and operant conditioning, the cognitive approach on information processing and the psychodynamic approach on the unconscious. With regard to methodology the behavioural and cognitive perspectives use scientific or empirical methods whereas the psychodynamic approach relies on interpretations based on psychodynamic concepts. Teachers should be aware that the causes of a given behaviour are often described according to the perspective a person decides to adopt. It is often necessary to consider the possibility that a given behaviour is the result of a number of causes (multi-factorial), some immediate and some remote, rather than there being one simple cause. Alternatively one cause can produce a number of different behaviours.

Teachers should not therefore underestimate the complexity of causation and should be open-minded about the causes of given behaviours. Indeed, with particular cases causation may be unknown but this does not necessarily preclude effective intervention.

It is often useful to consider the causes of behavioural problems in terms of personal and contextual predisposing, precipitating and perpetuating causes. Consideration of these factors facilitates formulation and intervention.

Relativity and subjectivity of perceptions of behaviour

What constitutes a behavioural problem can vary according to differing perceptions depending on social context, moral codes, cultural norms and historical periods. Therefore it can be the case that a teacher's judgement may disagree with other teachers' judgements because of different social contexts, moral codes or levels of tolerance.

The validity and effectiveness of different perspectives

There has been and continues to be disagreement over the relative validity and effectiveness of different approaches, e.g. the behavioural, cognitive and psychodynamic approaches. This disagreement has occurred because of the different theoretical underpinnings of the approaches and difficulties surrounding empirical and methodological evaluation. Some have adopted integrated or eclectic approaches. For practical purposes teachers should be guided by pragmatic considerations. Furthermore some have stated that the effectiveness of each of the approaches depends on non-specific factors related to the attributes of the person undertaking the interventions, e.g. warmth and genuineness.

The biological and biochemical bases of behaviour

In recent years biological and biochemical explanations for particular categories of behaviour have gained greater salience. The link between medical or organic conditions and behaviour is being explored, e.g. the influence of neurotransmitters (serotonin and dopamine), the effects of neurological or hormonal dysfunctions and the side effects of psychoactive drugs. Some behavioural problems are now seen as having a biological basis, e.g. ADHD, and are treated through drug therapy, the use of Ritalin. Teachers should note that in the case of ADHD, treatment does not preclude the use of behavioural methods as an adjunct.

The genetic and environmental influences on behaviour

Controversy has occurred and still occurs over the relative contributions of heredity and the environment to behaviour. However, most would agree that problem behaviour is the result of an interaction between a genetic predisposition and the environment. Currently there is an increased emphasis on researching the influence of heredity on emotional and behavioural problems through behavioural genetics.

Behavioural genetics investigates the behavioural differences in a specific population with a view to explaining behaviour in terms of genetic and environmental differences. This approach studies heritability (variation in a trait explained by heredity), shared environments (e.g. parental rearing practices) and non-shared environments (e.g. peer groups). The methodology is one based on twin and adoption studies. Certain disorders are seen as having a genetic component, e.g. autism and ADHD.

Determining the degree of genetic influence on behaviour has been a contentious issue and some research purporting to have established a genetic influence on a given type of behaviour has not been replicated. Polarisation has occurred with some claiming that behaviour is genetically determined and others that it is environmentally determined.

Currently behaviour is seen as resulting from interactions between genetic and environmental influences. Teachers should note that the assumption of genetic influence on behaviour does not preclude behavioural change.

The epidemiology or prevalence of behavioural problems

The degree of prevalence for a given behavioural problem depends on the criteria employed. However, it is agreed that behavioural problems are more prevalent than emotional problems and that behavioural problems are more prevalent among boys than girls and emotional problems more prevalent among girls. When the prevalence of a given problem is agreed there may be disagreement over the reasons for the prevalence, e.g. over-representation of particular ethnic groups in certain educational statistics.

Furthermore questions may be raised as to whether there has been under or over-diagnosis of specific behavioural problems. For example, some maintain that in the UK there has been under-diagnosis of ADHD compared to the USA. Teachers should be aware that their estimations of the number of students with behaviour problems may vary with their criteria and as a result may differ from the estimations of other professionals.

Situations and/or traits

Issues arise in relation to the consistency and inconsistency of behaviour and therefore its predictability. Trait theorists argue that there are personality traits that influence behaviour. Traits are regarded as stable, internal predispositions that influence behaviour across all contexts. Behaviour is seen as being predictable and consistent once these traits are known. Situationists regard traits as relatively unimportant in comparison with the influence of situations in predicting behaviour. External events are seen as bringing about consistent behaviour. Interactionists regard behaviour as being the product or result of interactions between traits and situations, i.e. situational factors are seen as moderating the influence of trait factors.

Behaviour is seen as predictable if there is knowledge of both traits and situations. In order to change behaviour knowledge of people's traits and their responses to given situations would be required.

Ethical concerns

Ethical concerns appear when people have concerns or fears over what they perceive as the basis of a particular perspective. Some concerns arise over controlling behaviour and others over the suppression of feelings.

For example, some regard the use of behaviour modification techniques as authoritarian and some regard the use of psychoanalytic approaches as lacking sufficient scientific validity to justify their use. It is important for teachers to have an accurate understanding of a given perspective and to be clear as to what they find ethically objectionable about a given approach.

Acknowledgements

First edition (1995)

The first edition of this book is based on the 'Perspectives on Behaviour' course which is an accredited EBD module of the Advanced Diploma in Special Educational Needs, of the University of London Institute of Education. We would specially like to acknowledge Brahm Norwich (at that time Responsible Tutor for the accredited module at the University of London Institute of Education).

The course at that time was delivered by Harry Ayers, Don Clarke and Anne Murray (members of the Tower Hamlets Support for Learning Service) and Brahm Norwich.

We are indebted to the course participants and teachers in the London Borough of Tower Hamlets for their contributions, time and encouragement. We thank pupils of schools in Tower Hamlets for their illustrations and also thank the following speakers on the course: Paul Cooper (now at the University of Cambridge, Institute of Education), Brahm Norwich (now at the University of Exeter) and Heather Geddes (member of the Forum for the Advancement of Educational Therapy and Therapeutic Teaching – FAETT – now known as the Caspari Foundation).

We would also like to acknowledge Martin Bonathan (SEN Policy Advisor, Birmingham LEA) who, as previous Head of Service Development at the Tower Hamlets Support for Learning Service, negotiated the original course module; and to thank the London Borough of Tower Hamlets LEA for their support in enabling us to write this book. Finally we would like to thank Liz Vickerie (Director) and teachers of the Tower Hamlets Support for Learning Service for their contributions and encouragement.

Second edition (2000)

The second edition is based on the first edition but has been revised and expanded to include additional perspectives. We wish to acknowledge the contributions of all those who supported and encouraged us in writing the first edition so enabling us to produce the second. We particularly wish to thank the London Borough of Tower Hamlets Local Education Authority.

Why use this book?

This book is a practical guide to the following eight perspectives on behaviour (see Comparison grid, p. xv–xvi):

- **biological** – focusing on biological and biochemical processes in accounting for behaviour;

- **behavioural** (or behaviourist) – focusing on overt, observable and measurable behaviours and their reinforcement in accounting for behaviour;

- **cognitive** (or cognitive-behavioural) – focusing on cognitive processes (beliefs, attitudes, expectations and attributions) in accounting for behaviour; combines both the cognitive and the behavioural perspective;

- **social learning** – focusing on observational learning, perceived self-efficacy and expectancies in accounting for behaviour;

- **psychodynamic** – focusing on unconscious conflicts in early childhood as accounting for current behaviour;

- **humanistic** – focusing on low self-esteem and problems in coping with and exploring feelings in accounting for behaviour;

- **ecosystemic** – focusing on positive and negative interactions between teachers and students within the school and those that externally affect the school; these interactions are seen as accounting for behaviour;

- **ecological** – focusing on the influence of systems and the environment in accounting for behaviour.

The aim of the book is to enable the reader to develop a structured approach to emotional and behavioural problems by drawing on one or more of the above perspectives.

It is helpful to plan interventions through a **five-stage model**:

- **identification** of the student as a cause for concern or *why* this student;

- **assessment** of the student's problem or *what* it is;

- **formulation** of the student's problem or *why* it happens;

- **intervention** or *ways* of dealing with the problem;

- **evaluation** of the intervention or its *effectiveness*.

The following model is a **general schema** that applies to the biological, behavioural, cognitive-behavioural, social learning, psychodynamic, humanistic, ecosystemic and ecological perspectives.

In terms of the schema, in the fullest sense, the psychodynamic perspective requires a specialised training that readers may not possess. However, an understanding of the psychodynamic approach will enable the reader to reflect on how student behaviour can be affected by unconscious processes and therefore be in a position to modify their own classroom practice in accordance with some of the broader ideas.

PERSPECTIVE SCHEMA	BEHAVIOURAL	COGNITIVE	SOCIAL LEARNING	ECOSYSTEMIC
Theoretical basis:	Classical /operant conditioning.	Cognitive schemas/ appraisal/information processing.	Reciprocal determinism.	Systems/ subsystems/ family therapy.
Model of person:	Behaviour results from learning.	Behaviour mediated through cognition.	Behaviour is influenced by per-ceived self-efficacy/ expectations.	Behaviour is the product of interactions.
Assessment basis:	Overt, observable, measurable behaviour.	Thoughts, beliefs, attitudes, inferences, attributions.	Efficacy/outcome expectations.	Interaction within and between subsystems. Interpretations of behaviour.
Assessment procedure:	Observation schedules, checklists, rating scales, profiles and ABC	Self-monitoring logs, self-reports, diaries and ABC.	Self-monitoring, self-report.	Interviews, observation, analysis of interpretations.
Formulation basis:	Reinforcement of problem behaviour.	Cognitive processes mediate problem behaviours.	Efficacy/outcome expectations mediate behaviour.	Negative interactions result in self-perpetuating cycles.
Formulation:	Problem behaviour caused by maladaptive learning.	Problem behaviour is influenced by maladaptive cognition.	Problem behaviour is influenced by negative efficacy/ outcome expectations.	Problem behaviour is the result of negative interactions/ interpretations.
Intervention basis:	Changing overt, observable, measurable, behaviour.	Changing maladaptive cognition.	Changing negative efficacy/outcome expectations.	Initiating/maintaining positive interactions.
Intervention strategies:	Reinforcement programmes, extinction, time-out, response cost, contracts, token economy, social skills training.	Problem-solving training, self-control, self-instruction, stress-inoculation training, re-attribution training	Modelling, coping skills, observational learning.	Reframing, sleuthing, symptom prescription, positive connotation of function and motive.
Evaluation basis:	Changes in overt, observable behaviours.	Adaptive changes in cognitive processes.	Changes in efficacy/ outcome expectations.	Changes in interactions/ interpretations.
Evaluation:	Comparison of behavioural change with baseline.	Increase in problem-solving, self-management, reattribution.	Increase in self-efficacy.	New cycles of positive interactions.
COMPARISON OF THE PERSPECTIVES				

PERSPECTIVE SCHEMA	BIOLOGICAL	ECOLOGICAL	PSYCHODYNAMIC	HUMANISTIC
Theoretical basis:	Genetic, neurological and physiological processes.	Social and physical environments.	Unconscious processes seeking resolution of psychic conflict, e.g. ego defences. Unconscious phantasy influences behaviour	Phenomenology/ subjective meanings/ perceptions/feelings.
Model of person:	Medical model. Genetics, brain chemistry and hormones influence behaviour.	Behaviour results from person– environment interaction.	Behaviour is determined by unconscious processes.	Self-actualising person. Fully-functioning person.
Assessment basis:	Neurotransmitters, physiological and hormonal functioning.	Person–environment interactions.	Ego defences unconscious phantasy; internal working model(s).	Self-concept/self-esteem. Actual/ideal self. Focus on feelings.
Assessment procedure:	Psychometric testing, neuropsychological testing, psycho-physiological measurement and brain imaging. Interviews.	Observation, self-report questionnaires and attitude surveys.	Projective techniques, transference-relationship; defences/ unconscious phantasies inferred	Rapport. Q-sort. Repertory grid. Lawseq questionnaire. Classroom observation.
Formulation basis:	Brain biochemistry or hormones.	Person– environment interactions.	Unresolved unconscious conflicts/phantasies/ inapropriate internal working models manifest in emotional and behavioural difficulties	Personal change/ growth/self-esteem/ feelings/self-understanding.
Formulation:	Problem behaviours are caused in part by genetic predisposition and through imbalances in neurotransmitters and hormones.	Problem behaviour is the result of negative person–environment interactions.	Problem behaviour caused by unresolved unconscious conflicts/ phantasies/internal working model arousing unconscious anxiety and ego defences	Problem behaviour results from low self-esteem/difficulties with feelings.
Intervention basis:	Rectifying neuro-transmitter and hormonal imbalances.	Changing person-environment interactions.	Facilitating insight; strengthening the ego	Self-concept/ self-esteem development. Personal resources.
Intervention strategies:	Drug therapy.	Modifying the social and physical environments, changing perceptions, attitudes and expectations.	Interpretation of resistance and defences or unconscious phantasy in and through the transference-relationship	Addressing Maslow's hierarchy of needs.
Evaluation basis:	Changes in cognitive processes and behaviour.	Changes in social and physical environments. Changes in perceptions, attitudes and expectations.	Insight into unconscious conflict; ego strength	Changes in self-concept. Changes in self-esteem. Changes in feelings.
Evaluation:	Positive changes in cognition and behaviour.	Positive change in environments, in perceptions and behaviour.	Increased insight and ego strength.	Positive changes in self-concept/self-esteem/feelings.
COMPARISON OF THE PERSPECTIVES				

Introduction

General schema

A **general schema** is a guide that enables teachers to adopt a structured approach towards dealing with behaviour problems regardless of the chosen perspective. It can take the following form:

1. assessment
2. formulation
3. intervention
4. evaluation

Assessment phase

Describing the student's problem

BIOLOGICAL
: *Assessment techniques:* behavioural genetics, psychometric and neuropsychological testing, psychophysiological measurement, brain imaging (PET, CT and MRI) and brain anatomy.

BEHAVIOURAL
: *Assessment techniques:* direct observation using event sampling and frequency counts; conducting interviews, using questionnaires, rating scales, checklists and an ABC or functional analysis.

COGNITIVE
: *Assessment techniques:* using interviews to explore beliefs, attitudes and attributions; using self-monitoring, e.g. keeping a log or diary: using self-rating scales, time-event charts, self-report questionnaires; using an ABC analysis that includes beliefs as well as antecedents, behaviours and consequences.

SOCIAL LEARNING
: *Assessment techniques:* using interviews and self-report questionnaires to explore perceived self-efficacy and expectancies.

PSYCHODYNAMIC
: *Assessment techniques:* using free association, using transference and counter-transference, interpreting dreams, using projective methods, e.g. the Rorschach or inkblot test, the Thematic Apperception Test (TAT) or story-telling tests; interpreting drawings, playing with toys and using interviews.

HUMANISTIC
: *Assessment techniques:* using sociometry, self-report, actual and ideal self-questionnaires, the Q-sort and the personal construct repertory grid.

ECOSYSTEMIC   *Assessment techniques:* data collection, i.e. interviews, questionnaires and surveys, on the attitudes, expectations and interactions between teachers, pupils and significant others, and on aspects of the student's social environment; sociometry (a method of investigating the relationships between students) and the use of systematic observation, checklists and rating scales.

ECOLOGICAL   *Assessment techniques:* data collection, i.e. interviews, questionnaires, surveys, observations on the grouping of students, seating arrangements, student perception and teacher expectation, classroom and pastoral organisation.

Formulation phase

Why are the student's problems occurring?

BIOLOGICAL   This perspective formulates in terms of the ways in which behaviour problems are influenced by heredity and by other biological processes, e.g. neurotransmitter malfunctions.

BEHAVIOURAL   This perspective formulates in terms of the ways in which behaviour problems are being triggered and maintained through positive and negative reinforcement.

COGNITIVE   This perspective formulates in terms of the ways in which behaviour problems are influenced by and associated with a student's patterns of thoughts, beliefs, attitudes and attributions.

SOCIAL LEARNING   This perspective formulates in terms of the ways in which behaviour problems are brought about through a student's observational learning, modelling and perceived self-efficacy.

PSYCHODYNAMIC   This perspective formulates in terms of the ways in which behaviour problems stem from unconscious emotional conflicts experienced in early childhood. These conflicts emerge in the form of emotional and behavioural difficulties.

HUMANISTIC   This perspective formulates in terms of the ways in which behaviour problems result from poor self-esteem and difficulties in coping with feelings.

ECOSYSTEMIC   This perspective formulates in terms of the ways in which behaviour problems result from interactions between teachers, parents, students and peers. A behaviour problem is not seen as located solely within the student, but rather as a product of negative interactions between the student, teachers, parents and peers.

ECOLOGICAL   This perspective formulates in terms of the ways in which behaviour problems are brought about through interactions between students and their social and physical environments. Students influence the environment and environments influence students. Behaviour problems are contextual in that they cannot be seen in isolation from their setting.

Intervention phase

Methods of changing a student's behaviour

BIOLOGICAL   Interventions are based on the premiss that a student's problems are the result of adverse biological and neuropsychological processes. Drug therapy or biological treatment is used, e.g. Ritalin for ADHD.

BEHAVIOURAL   Interventions are based on the premiss that students need to learn appropriate or to unlearn inappropriate behaviour. Operant techniques are applied, e.g. positive and negative reinforcement, extinction, contingency contracting, token economy, response cost and time-out.

COGNITIVE   Interventions are based on the premiss that students lack verbal mediation strategies for developing reflective self-control, e.g. problem-solving training, self-instructional training, stress-inoculation and attribution retraining that can be delivered through modelling, role play and behavioural contingencies (examples being self-rewarding, positive self-statements and rewards for accurate self-evaluation).

SOCIAL LEARNING   Interventions are based on the idea that students experiencing behavioural problems need to acquire new behaviours and increase their perceived self-efficacy through observational learning and modelling.

PSYCHODYNAMIC   Interventions use various methods aimed at resolving or reducing unconscious conflicts, fears and anxieties that interfere with the student's appropriate engagement with the learning situation. When successful, the emotional energy hitherto tied up in unconscious conflicts or anxiety is released and enables the student to direct this energy towards making progress in learning.

HUMANISTIC   Interventions are based on the idea that students are experiencing low self-esteem and that they also have difficulties in coping with their feelings towards others. Various approaches are used with the aim of raising the student's self-esteem, encouraging student self-actualisation and improving the student's relationships with others. Students are encouraged through person-centred counselling to develop positive self-concepts, to recognise and acknowledge feelings and to relate positively to others. Person-centred counselling is based on genuineness or congruence, unconditional positive regard and empathy.

ECOSYSTEMIC   Interventions are based on the idea that students' negative interactions with parents, teachers and peers need to be addressed through the use of specific ecosystemic techniques, e.g. reframing, positive connotation of motive, positive connotation of function and symptom prescription.

ECOLOGICAL   Interventions are based on addressing student–environment interactions. The physical and social environment needs to be changed or modified at different levels through e.g. home–school liaison, implementing effective whole-school behaviour policies, improving classroom management and reorganisation of the pastoral and learning systems.

Evaluation phase

Did the intervention produce a change in the student's behaviour?

BIOLOGICAL
Evaluation is based on the effects of drug therapy on a student's cognitive processes and behaviours.

BEHAVIOURAL
Evaluation is based on observation of a student's specific target behaviours over the period of the intervention. A pre-intervention baseline (of the student's typical behaviour) is established to enable a comparison to be made with the student's subsequent behaviour after the intervention has been introduced. Other experimental designs, e.g. reversal and multiple baseline designs, can be used to test whether a change in the student's behaviour is the result of the intervention or some other influence. Teachers' and parents' perceptions can also be ascertained.

COGNITIVE
Evaluation is based on changes that have occurred in the student's beliefs, attitudes and attributions that are associated with a change in the student's behaviour. These cognitive changes can be evaluated through the use of self-reports, interviews with teachers, parents and students and direct observation of behaviour (as above).

SOCIAL LEARNING
Evaluation is based on identifying changes in a student's perceived self-efficacy and expectancies that lead to changes in baseline behaviour.

PSYCHODYNAMIC
Evaluation is based on inferences made by therapists or counsellors as to positive changes in a student's cognition and behaviour that result from resolution of that student's unconscious conflicts and anxieties. In addition use is made of projective methods for the same purpose, e.g. Rorschach or TAT. Experimental designs have also been used to evaluate psychodynamic approaches but they are difficult to test.

HUMANISTIC
Interventions are based on the idea that students are experiencing low self-esteem and that they also have difficulties in coping with their feelings towards others. Various approaches are used with the aim of raising the student's self-esteem, encouraging student self-actualisation and improving the student's relationships with others. Students are encouraged through person-centred counselling to develop positive self-concepts, to recognise and acknowledge feelings and to relate positively to others. Person-centred counselling is based on genuineness or congruence, unconditional positive regard and empathy.

ECOSYSTEMIC
Evaluation is based on observation, self-reports, interviews, surveys and questionnaires. The aim is to establish that the introduction of ecosystemic techniques has resulted in positive changes in interactions between teachers, parents and peers.

ECOLOGICAL
Evaluation is based on observation, surveys and questionnaires that seek to establish that changes in the physical and social environment contribute to positive changes in student behaviour.

1 The biological perspective

This perspective is included solely for information for teachers so that they are aware of how developments in the field of biology relate to particular types of behaviour problems, most notably ADHD and autism.

Definition

The biological perspective considers mental disorders to have underlying physical or organic causes, e.g. schizophrenia. Mental disorders are characterised in terms of the medical model, which include pathology, symptoms, diagnosis and prognosis. There are various approaches within the perspective:

- **Behavioural genetics:** sees mental disorders and other behaviours as being significantly influenced by a person's heredity. The aim of this approach through family comparisons and twin, adoption and linkage studies is to determine the degree to which behaviour is influenced by genes and the degree to which it is influenced by the environment. Many genetically influenced disorders appear to fit a diathesis-stress model, i.e. genetic makeup together with environmental stress produce a disorder. Behavioural genetics has evoked controversy in the form of disagreements over the results of twin and other studies and the replication of research.

- **Brain biochemistry:** sees some mental disorders and other behaviours as being influenced by abnormal biochemical reactions in parts of the nervous system. In particular certain types of neurotransmitters are believed to play a part in some mental disorders. Neurotransmitters are chemicals that facilitate electrical impulses between nerves in the brain. A number of neurotransmitters have been put forward as having a role in mental disorders, e.g. dopamine and serotonin. This is thought to be in terms of an excess or a deficit of a particular neurotransmitter. Psychopharmacology uses drugs to treat mental disorders which are thought to be influenced by imbalances of neurotransmitters. There are drug treatments for anxiety, depression and psychoses. Although these drugs can have positive effects they may also have unpleasant side effects, may not work for all patients and may treat the symptoms rather than the cause.

- **Brain anatomy**: sees some mental disorders and other behaviours as being influenced by abnormalities in the anatomy or structure of the brain. For example, schizophrenia has been connected to enlarged ventricles in the brain. Psychosurgery, the use of surgery to treat mental disorders, has a controversial history, e.g. prefrontal lobotomy. However it has been used in the form of a surgical procedure, cingulotomy, to disrupt pathways in the brain in order to decrease severe emotional stress as in obsessive-compulsive disorder. Usually these are measures of last resort where other treatments have failed.

- **Endocrinology**: sees some mental disorders and other behaviours as being influenced by dysfunctions of the endocrine system in the form of hormonal imbalances, e.g. low levels of activity in the thyroid can result in anxiety.

Evaluation of the biological perspective

This perspective tends to a reductionist viewpoint when it reduces mental disorders to being simply the result of abnormal biological processes. Cause and effect may be difficult to disentangle, as biochemical abnormalities may be the effect rather than the cause of a disorder. Furthermore one cannot necessarily conclude that the drug treatment of a disorder indicates it is a lack of that drug in the brain that is the cause of the disorder. This perspective also tends to emphasise the importance of genetic causes for disorders rather than environmental causes. Controversy has arisen over the degree to which heredity contributes to disorders and other behaviour. There appears to be an acceptance that both nature and nurture play a part but disagreement over how much.

Drug treatment is not always successful given that individual responses do differ, some benefiting, others showing adverse side effects and others displaying no improvement. In some cases symptoms are reduced but the causes remain. However, many people have benefited from drug therapy, for example in reducing the positive symptoms of schizophrenia, e.g. delusions and hallucinations. In the case of ADHD children have reduced their hyperactivity through taking the drug Ritalin.

Teachers should not conclude that all behaviour is biologically determined and therefore behaviour is inevitably fixed and unchangeable. Even where there is an assumed biological influence on behaviour this does not preclude psychological intervention, e.g. behavioural methods in the case of ADHD.

Biological assessment

Biological assessment focuses on brain dysfunctions or abnormalities and uses a variety of methods such as brain imaging techniques, neurochemical approaches, neuropsychological tests and psychophysiological measurements.

- *Brain imaging techniques* such as computerised axial tomography (CAT scans), magnetic resonance imaging (MRI) and positron emission tomography (PET scans) are used to investigate brain abnormalities and linkage with mental disorders.

- *Neurochemical approaches* depend on detecting and analysing the levels of neurotransmitters in the brain by for example looking for the metabolites of those neurotransmitters. The aim is to study the links between neurotransmitter levels and mental disorders.

- *Neuropsychological tests* are used to help assess mental disorders that are related to brain abnormalities; for example, the Halstead-Reitan battery of tests and the Luria-Nebraska battery are used to assess brain damage.

- *Psychophysiological assessment* measures electrical and chemical changes that are related to psychological states. Examples are electrocardiagrams, electro-encephalograms (EEGs) and electromyograms.

With regard to biological assessment it is important to be aware that there are problems in interpreting the assessment results and that there is no necessary one-to-one correspondence between results of scans and tests and a particular psychological abnormality.

Biological treatment

Given that the biological perspective focuses on the links between brain biochemistry and mental disorders, then treatment is through application of the appropriate drug therapy. For example, anxiolytics (sedatives and tranquillisers) are used to treat anxiety and phobias; anti-depressants are used to treat depression and eating disorders; and anti-psychotics are used to treat schizophrenia.

It should be remembered that drug therapy can have adverse side effects related to the drug prescribed and that specific drugs do not necessarily work for everyone suffering from a particular mental disorder

ADHD (Attention Deficit Hyperactivity Disorder): an example of the biological approach to a behavioural disorder

Classification

This disorder or syndrome is characterised as one where an individual manifests overactivity, impulsivity and inattention. Children who suffer from this disorder will probably experience social and educational failure. Problems among the majority affected can continue into late adolescence and for some into adulthood. Adolescents affected are at risk of developing a conduct disorder and becoming substance abusers and delinquents.

A physician or psychiatrist using a diagnostic manual, DSM IV or ICD 10, diagnoses ADHD. It is stated in both manuals that symptoms must be present in two settings, e.g. at home and school, for a diagnosis to be valid. Achenbach's Child Behaviour Checklist system can also be used to make a diagnosis.

The clinical characteristics are a brief attention span, distractibility, inability to foresee the consequences of one's actions, antisocial behaviour, excitability, risk-taking and poor school performance. There are problems with relationships with parents, teachers and peers. There are subtypes of ADHD, the inattentive and the hyperactive-impulsive. The hyperactive-impulsive subtype is characterised by extreme overactivity and aggression resulting in behavioural difficulties in school.

Depending on the diagnostic criteria prevalence rates for ADHD can vary from 1% to 19%. The prevalence rate is higher for boys than for girls and greater in pre-adolescence than in late adolescence. There is quite a high co-morbidity of ADHD with conduct and emotional disorders.

Causes

The biological perspective considers genetics, brain dysfunctions, neurotransmitter problems, diet and underarousal to be key factors in the causes of ADHD. Genetics suggests that children with ADHD have a predisposition to develop the disorder. Brain imaging techniques have not detected brain abnormalities and neurological assessment has not detected a pattern of cognitive processing problems in children with ADHD. The neurotransmitter hypothesis considers the symptoms of ADHD to be associated with neurotransmitter malfunctioning. Drug therapy with psychostimulants like Ritalin (methylphenidate) is believed to have a positive effect on abnormal neurotransmitter functioning. About 60% to 90% of children respond well to drug treatment but the positive effects disappear once it is terminated. Particular children with allergies to specific foods who have ADHD may improve if put on diets that exclude those foods. The underarousal theory suggests that children with ADHD are underaroused and as a result seek stimuli. Psychophysiological tests have indicated reduced psychophysiological responses to new stimuli.

Other, non-biological theories have been suggested in terms of specific deficits such as an inability to maintain attention, difficulties in inhibiting overactivity, an impulsivity that hinders the application of appropriate social and cognitive coping strategies and an inability to follow rules.

Assessment

The assessment or diagnosis of ADHD requires information to be obtained in both the home and school setting. It is suggested that a multidisciplinary assessment be undertaken in terms of gathering information on ability, educational attainment, behaviour and medical background. Checklists are recommended for assessing behaviour in school and in the home, e.g. Achenbach's (1991) Child Behaviour Checklist system. Paediatric medical assessment is also considered useful for identifying biological predisposing factors.

Formulation

The formulation will include information from the school and home, psychological tests and checklists and paediatric medicals. This information will be combined in a formulation.

Intervention

The biological intervention is through drug therapy, namely the prescription of psychostimulant medication, e.g. methylphenidate (Ritalin). Side effects can happen, e.g. loss of appetite and sleep disturbance and, in rare instances, tics. The drug is effective in most cases of children with ADHD. However, if the drug is discontinued the improvements end. Non-biological interventions include behavioural and cognitive methods. Operant techniques such as positive reinforcement programmes combined with response cost and time-out can be complementary to drug therapy. Teachers and parents can be trained in the use of operant techniques. Cognitive interventions include self-instructional training and anger management training; these too can be complementary to drug therapy.

Conclusion

The assessment and treatment of ADHD is from the biological perspective. Assessment is multi-disciplinary through medical and psychological approaches. The main cause of ADHD is believed to be disordered brain biochemistry. Drugs like Ritalin significantly improve concentration and behaviour. They can have side effects and if the drug is discontinued behaviour deteriorates. Other interventions are effective but usually in conjunction with drug therapy. ADHD provides a clear instance of the effectiveness of the biological approach to a behavioural disorder. However, interventions based on other perspectives, e.g. the behavioural and the cognitive, are also effective particularly combined with drug therapy.

Guidance for teachers

- Awareness of the biological perspective is essential in that emotional and behavioural difficulties may be in part or in full the result of neurobiological or physiological dysfunctions. Furthermore medical conditions and the side effects of drug treatments themselves may have negative behavioural consequences. Examination of medical records if possible may throw light on emotional and behavioural problems.

- A biological or genetic predisposition to an emotional or behavioural problem in itself does not necessarily preclude the influence of other non-biological factors, e.g. family conflict.

- Biological treatments do not preclude the use of other interventions, e.g. behavioural methods can be a useful adjunct to the prescription of Ritalin in the case of ADHD.

Autism: a disorder believed to have an underlying biological basis

Classification

This disorder describes children who manifest difficulties in social interaction, social communication and language development and who also display repetitive, obsessive and restricted patterns of behaviour. It is an example of a pervasive developmental disorder and was first identified by L. Kanner in 1943. It has a prevalence rate of 2–5 per 10,000 and it is more common in boys than girls, the ratio being 4:1. Intellectually about 75% of autistic children score below 70 on intelligence tests. Some children have high levels of achievement in specific areas, e.g. musical memory. Asperger's syndrome is similar to autism but is different in that there is no language delay or intellectual impairment.

With autism there are social, linguistic and behavioural deficits. There are impairments in social and peer relationships, attachment problems and a lack of empathy. Language development is delayed and characterised by echolalia, neologisms and pronoun reversal. Behaviour is characterised by stereotyped, repetitive, ritualistic, obsessive actions and restricted interests. There is often a desire to preserve routines and avoidance of change. L. Wing (1993) believes that autism can be classified into three sub-groups: aloof, passive and active-but-odd type.

Causes

There are three main theories of autism: psychodynamic, cognitive and biological. Current research points to a neurobiological cause for autism that manifests itself in the form of specific cognitive deficits. Genetic, intrauterine environment and congenital factors have been implicated along with some form of brain abnormality. Fragile X syndrome is associated with autism.

Assessment

Among the most common assessment methods for autism are:

- interviews with parents and teachers using adaptive behaviour scales;
- intelligence testing using WISC-III;
- functional analysis of challenging behaviour.

Formulation

Autism is currently regarded as being caused by neurobiological factors that result in cognitive deficits.

Intervention

1. *Structured teaching* (TEACHH approach, Schopler, 1997) The aim of this approach is to build on the strengths of the child, e.g. visual processing, rote learning and special interests. Highly structured work routines are implemented in a distraction free context.
2. *Behavioural approach* The aim of this approach is to deal with the challenging behaviours manifested in aggression and self-injury. Operant (positive reinforcement) and modelling techniques have been used to encourage autistic children to talk and play with other children.
3. *Biological approach* Drugs such as haloperidol, fenfluramine and naltrexone have been used but have not significantly affected the core symptoms.

Conclusion

Autism is believed to be a neurobiological disorder where biological treatment or drug therapy has only a limited effect on the core symptoms. Non-biological interventions, e.g. TEACHH and behavioural techniques, have proven useful but they address specific symptoms rather than provide a cure.

2 The behavioural perspective

The behavioural model

The focus of this perspective is on a person's overt, observable and measurable behaviour. It excludes all reference to cognitive or unconscious processes. This approach is based on the theory that an individual's overt and observable behaviour unless genetically influenced is the result of that individual's learning.

Learning occurs through Classical and Operant conditioning, the result of environmental influences. An individual's behaviour is the result of that individual's past and present learning experiences. The main focus would be on current environmental events that are assumed to be controlling, that is triggering and maintaining, the observed behaviour. This approach adopts a scientific or empirical methodology that emphasises structure and objectivity with regard to assessment, formulation, intervention and evaluation.

Classical conditioning (I. Pavlov)

Classical conditioning occurs when conditioned associations occur between stimuli and responses. Pavlov saw behaviours as chains of conditioned associations.

CS———UR   (bell elicits attention)

US———CR   (food is presented every time after the bell is rung and then salivation occurs)

CS———CR   (bell eventually elicits salivation without food being presented).

CS = conditioned stimulus
UR = unconditioned response
US = unconditioned stimulus
CR = conditioned response

In this example, the dog has learnt to salivate to the sound of the bell as well as to the food. However if food never follows after the sound of the bell finishes, the dog will cease salivating at the sound of the bell.

As another example, a teacher shouts at a student eliciting that student's attention. The student stops talking and the teacher points at the same time as, or just after, shouting. The student therefore associates pointing with shouting. The teacher points at the student without shouting and eventually the student stops talking and pays attention in response to the pointing alone. The student has thus become conditioned to pointing.

Pavlov's conclusion was that many emotional and behavioural responses were the result of conditioning.

Behaviourism (J. B. Watson)

Behaviourism saw the study of behaviour as requiring a scientific approach based on objectivity and experimentation with regard to overt, observable and measurable behaviour. Introspection was seen as an unscientific methodology. Fear responses were described as being the product of conditioning. Watson induced a fear or phobic response in an 11-month child. His example was as follows: a child does not fear rats but fears loud sounds; Watson therefore makes banging sound when a rat is presented and the child eventually fears the rat because fear-inducing sound becomes associated with the appearance of the rat. This fear generalises to other stimuli that have rat-like characteristics.

Watson did not regard thought processes as having any causal impact on an individual's behaviour and did not consider thought processes to be directly observable. He also saw maladaptive behaviour as the product of a person's history of conditioning. In his view, observable symptoms are the behaviours and there are no underlying causes such as unconscious conflict.

Operant conditioning (B. F. Skinner)

Operant conditioning occurs where behaviours are shaped by environmental stimuli. A person is described as 'operating' on an environment that either does or does not respond. In particular operant conditioning occurs when an operant response is followed by a reinforcing stimulus that by itself increases the probability of the response happening again.

For example, students put their hand up rather than shouting out and the teacher praises the student on each occasion when the hand is raised and ignores the student when the student shouts out. The consequence of the teacher's praise is to reinforce pupils in raising their hand rather than shouting out. This happens repeatedly and students respond by increasing their hand-raising behaviour.

The behaviour of a person is simply those behaviours that have been reinforced over time. This idea was based on Thorndike's Law of Effect, i.e. behaviour that leads to satisfaction is strengthened; behaviour which is ignored or is unsatisfying is weakened. Skinner just saw an empirical Law of Effect: all that can be said is that a person's behaviour is observed being reinforced and that in all probability the behaviour will be repeated when reinforced over and over again. Behaviour therefore is reinforced by its consequences

Operant learning occurs when people learn when and how to respond, i.e. discriminate between stimuli in terms of those types of responses which do or do not receive reinforcement. In the instance mentioned above shouting does not receive reinforcement but raising a hand does; however, it could be the other way round since connections are only contingent. Students need to learn what types of responses are required for reinforcement to occur, i.e. the relevant contingencies and the timing and patterning of reinforcement or schedules of reinforcement.

Evaluation of the behavioural perspective

The behavioural perspective sees maladaptive behaviour as the product of past and current learning experiences although it does recognise the contribution that genetics makes to behaviour. Maladaptive behaviour can be unlearned and adaptive behaviour learned. The person's past is considered in terms of their learning history but current events are considered to be more influential. Maladaptive behaviour is simply seen as the pattern symptoms, there are no underlying causes and there is no 'symptom substitution'. When the symptoms disappear, the problem disappears with them. In terms of effectiveness the behavioural approach has been scientifically evaluated and is relatively effective across a range of emotional and behavioural problems, e.g. anxiety, phobias and different kinds of disruptive classroom behaviour. It can be used in conjunction with biological treatments, e.g. with drug therapy in the case of ADHD.

However, the behavioural perspective does not address problems where cognitive or psychodynamic factors might be involved in or responsible for maladaptive behaviour. Cognitive and unconscious processes are ignored. It does not consider underlying causes that may be operating but simply focuses on observable symptoms. It emphasises changing people's behaviours through external methods rather than through the person's own resources. People are therefore seen as passive recipients rather than active agents. Furthermore, the scientific basis of conditioning appears inadequate in certain respects. The idea of biological 'preparedness' appears necessary to explain why certain stimuli become the subjects of phobias and not others, e.g. snakes. Therefore biological constraints can limit the effects of conditioning. Finally, it is said that awareness is not simply an effect of conditioning but can be a cause of a person's behaviour, e.g. a person can choose to be reinforced or not.

Behavioural assessment

The basis

Behavioural assessment is based on a scientific methodology on what is overt and observable. Behaviour is considered to be relatively quantifiable in terms of latency, frequency, duration and severity or intensity. This type of assessment is concerned with maintaining objectivity. This means avoiding high levels of inference, speculation, bias and prejudice about behaviours and causes of behaviour. Behavioural assessment excludes reference to cognitive or psychodynamic factors. It also subscribes to a dimensional rather than a categorical approach to behaviour, i.e. seeing behaviour as lying along a continuum rather than being describable in terms of categories or labels. Behaviour is defined in functional terms, i.e. the functions it serves rather than what it describes. It is also defined relative to a given context or situation.

The aim of this form of assessment is to describe accurately the occurrence and sequence of overt and observable behaviours and the antecedents and consequences of those behaviours. Antecedents are the events immediately preceding given behaviours and consequences are events immediately following the behaviours. This takes the form of a functional or ABC analysis of behaviour, describing the pattern of antecedents and consequences.

Main principles

- Behavioural assessment involves identifying overt, observable and specific behaviours, e.g. a student's speech acts and off-task behaviours that are perceived as problematic by teachers or parents.

- Both excesses and deficits in behaviour are identified along with their appropriateness or inappropriateness relative to the context, e.g. the student spends too much time or too little time in class discussions in English and too much or too little time in movement in PE.

- Emphasis is placed on current patterns of observable behaviour rather than looking for causes in the distant or remote past, e.g. the student's existing off-task behaviour. However it should be noted that past learning behaviour could have a bearing on current learning behaviour, for example, in terms of the student's reinforcement history. There is a focus on factors that serve to set off the behaviours, called triggers, and factors that serve to maintain the behaviours over time. For example, teachers shouting at a student becomes a trigger and other students' expressed amusement at the student's antics, becomes a maintaining factor.

- Behavioural functional analysis concentrates on the context of the student's problem behaviours, e.g. if it is in the classroom, in most subjects, in the afternoons, at the end of the day and with certain other pupils. It also looks at what teachers and pupils say and do before the student's problem behaviours and what the student, other students and the teacher do and say afterwards.

- Behavioural assessment avoids using pre-determined labels or categories, preferring to see behaviour as lying along a continuum. Behaviour is described in terms of degrees of difference rather than kinds of difference. Labelling can stigmatise and it can also lead to concentration on the weaknesses rather than the strengths of a student.

- The main conclusion of an assessment should be the arrival at a formulation of the problem, i.e. a specific description of the problem behaviours, how they have developed, how they are being maintained and how they can be decreased or terminated. A formulation should lead to testable hypotheses resulting in long term objectives and short term targets. These targets are summed up in the acronym SMART, i.e.

S	PECIFIC
M	EASURABLE
A	CHIEVABLE
R	ELEVANT
T	IME-LIMITED

The methods used in behavioural assessment

Behaviours are assessed specifically in terms of latency, frequency, duration and severity or intensity. The aim is to arrive at a representative sample of current problem behaviours over a number of weeks. This sampling is undertaken in order to establish a behavioural pre-intervention baseline. This baseline is used as a benchmark or standard to allow comparison of behaviour in the future after an intervention has been implemented. The baseline forms a representative sample of behaviour, e.g. a student is observed over a two- or three-week period to be out of his or her seat on average ten times every hour over two weeks. The observed rate of out-of-seat behaviour can then be compared with the post-intervention rate. It should be noted that a statistical reduction in problem behaviour might not necessarily meet a particular teacher's success criteria.

- Latency refers to the length of time before a student performs the problem behaviour.
- Duration refers to the length of time the problem behaviour lasts.
- Frequency refers to the number of times the problem behaviour occurs during a particular period of time, e.g. the number of times students leave their seat.
- Intensity refers to a readiness to engage in the behaviour, its high frequency, its long duration and its high impact.

Behaviour frequency recording

Specific and discrete behaviours can be counted over a given period of time, e.g. the number of times in ten minutes a student shouts out to a teacher.

Interval recording

This refers to measuring problem behaviour by recording that behaviour during a specified block of time, which is divided into a number of short intervals, e.g. 15 seconds.

During the interval the problem behaviour (e.g. out-of-seat events) is regarded as having occurred or not occurred, e.g. a student may be observed for 15 second intervals over 20 minutes. The observer records if the student does or does not stay in his or her seat for the given interval. Interval scoring require the use of a sheet on which intervals are marked (see Figure 2.1 for a fixed interval sampling sheet) This approach enables an observer to record nearly all kinds of behaviours and the results can be worked out as a percentage of total time.

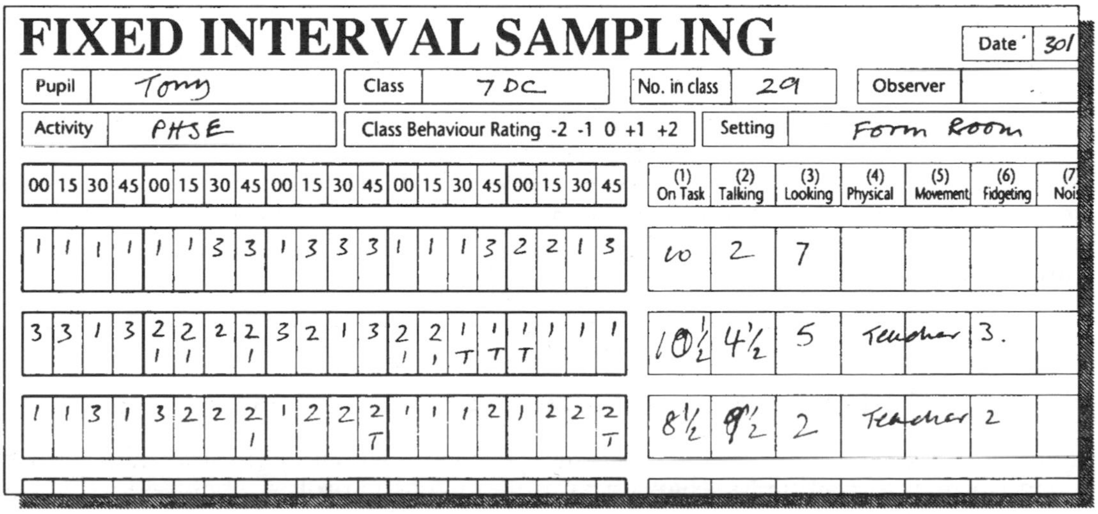

FIXED INTERVAL SAMPLING

Date 30/

Pupil Tony | Class 7 DC | No. in class 29 | Observer

Activity PHSE | Class Behaviour Rating -2 -1 0 +1 +2 | Setting Form Room

00	15	30	45	00	15	30	45	00	15	30	45	00	15	30	45	00	15	30	45
1	1	1	1	1	1	3	3	1	3	3	3	1	1	1	3	2	2	1	3
3	3	1	3	2 1	2 1	2	2 1	3	2	1	3	2 1	2 1	1 T	1 T	1 T	1	1	1
1	1	3	1	3	2	2	2 1	1	2	2	2 T	1	1	1	2	1	2	2	2 T

(1) On Task	(2) Talking	(3) Looking	(4) Physical	(5) Movement	(6) Fidgeting	(7) Noi
10	2	7				
10½	4½	5	Teacher		3.	
8½	9½	2	Teacher		2	

Figure 2.1 The fixed interval sampling sheet

Direct observation

Functional or ABC analysis is based on direct observation. Through the use of the ABC teachers can keep a running record of students' problem behaviours and the antecedents and consequences of those problem behaviours.

The ABC records can be collated and summarised in order to arrive at conclusions as to the patterns of students' problem behaviours, e.g. days, times, subjects and activities. These summaries should contribute to formulations, i.e. hypotheses that should lead to interventions that might decrease or terminate the problem behaviours.

In observing students, teachers can use behaviour frequency and interval recording sheets. These sheets can be annotated if necessary with additional observations at the time of recording.

Issues relating to observation

Ideally because of the variability of behaviour, a representative sample of behaviour should be obtained over an extended period, say two or three weeks. However, students' problem behaviours may be known to occur on particular days, at certain times and in specific contexts thus allowing economical observation.

Observation can be undertaken through using frequency, interval, duration and latency methods to record problem behaviours.

Teachers should be aware of various problems that can occur with the process of observation. Quite frequently students become aware they are being observed and as a result the observer's presence changes the students' behaviour (known as *reactivity*). However, this is usually temporary and may be eliminated as the students become habituated or accustomed to the observer's presence.

Observers should agree on the specific definitions of behaviour and when observing students agree on what they are observing (known as *inter-rater reliability*). There needs to be periodic checking that observers agree over what is being observed to avoid what is known as *behavioural drift*, that is, observers drifting away from the agreed definitions of specific behaviours. Observers should also be aware of any biases or prejudices that may contaminate their observations.

Assessment instruments

Teachers can make use of the checklists and profiles that enable them to record specific information about students' problem behaviours in a structured, comprehensive and systematic way; see Ayers *et al.* (1996) for recording instruments.

Behavioural interviewing

The aims of behavioural interviews are to:

- contribute information for a specific and accurate description of the student's problem behaviours;

- contribute information to achieve a formulation of the problem behaviours;

- contribute to an overall behavioural assessment of the student.

When interviewing the student the interviewer should:

- find out what events trigger and maintain the student's problem behaviours in both the home and school contexts;

- find out what rewards or punishments, if any, influence the student's behaviours.

When interviewing parents/carers the interviewer should:

- find out what they think triggers and maintains the student's problem behaviours in both the home and school contexts;

- find out what rewards or punishments, if any, influence the student's behaviours.

When interviewing teachers and other members of staff the interviewer should ascertain:

- what they think triggers and maintains the student's problem behaviours in both the home and school contexts;

- in particular the latency, frequency, duration and severity of the student's problem behaviours;

- the learning and behavioural strengths as well as the weaknesses of the student;

- the strategies and interventions used by teachers and the effectiveness of those interventions, particularly rewards and punishments.

The information provided by the student, parents and teachers should be collated and integrated into an overall behavioural assessment of the student.

The ABC Model of Analysis

This model provides a method of analysing behaviour:

A refers to the antecedent events, those observable events that immediately precede the student's problem behaviour;

B refers to the problem behaviour itself, i.e. what the student is actually doing in observable terms not what the teacher thinks or infers that the pupil is doing;

C refers to the consequences of the problem behaviour, those observable events that immediately follow on from the student's problem behaviour.

Besides the immediate or proximal events, it is also possible to identify remote or background antecedent events and consequences that contribute to the problem behaviour. These remote events and consequences are not observable in the immediate context but could be observed to influence the immediate situation (see Figure 2.2).

Date/time	Antecedents	Behaviour	Consequences
	Teacher shouts at student	Student shouts back	Other students laugh
	Asked to work on his own	Leaves seat	Sits on other student's seat
	Teacher leaves room	Student runs around the classroom	Other students run around as well

Figure 2.2 An example of ABC analysis

A Events occurring immediately prior to the student's problem behaviour may prompt that behaviour. The teacher needs to be aware of occurrences that trigger the pupil's problem behaviour and the consequences of the behaviour in terms of the student and other students. Antecedents are either immediate, e.g. the classroom situation, or background which include events at home. The main focus is on the immediate events. See Ayers *et al.* (1996) for greater detail and photocopiable forms.

B Teachers should identify and define clearly and accurately the observable problem behaviours.

C The immediate consequences for the student can be reinforcing or punishing. The teacher should be aware of aspects of classroom management and teaching that might be reinforcing the student appropriately or inappropriately. Other students might also be reinforcing the student's problem behaviour.

Remote or background antecedents might be reinforcing problem behaviours in the school but this does not necessarily mean that those antecedents must be changed in order for behaviour to change to occur in school.

It should be noted that the connections between antecedents, consequences and the problem behaviours are contingent or empirical, i.e. actually observed events.

Behavioural formulation

A behavioural formulation should be based on a behavioural assessment and consist of the following elements:

- a precise, clear and specific description of the problem behaviours;

- an hypothesis as to what events are triggering and maintaining the behaviours;

- an idea as to how these problems could be managed, i.e. an intervention that emerges from the formulation;

- an idea as to the likely outcome of the suggested intervention.

Example

John is a 10-year-old boy with reading difficulties, who is frequently out of his seat in the classroom (as measured through formal observation-fixed interval sampling). When presented with reading work by the teacher (an antecedent event), John leaves his seat and moves around the classroom talking to other pupils (problem behaviours) who laugh when he talks to them (consequence).

Through leaving his seat John avoids reading; he continues to avoid reading by staying out of his seat, in effect maintaining the problem behaviour (a formulation). John needs his reading skills improved through an appropriate reading programme along with paired reading, peer tutoring and mentoring (interventions focused on learning). He also needs a positive reinforcement programme that encourages him to stay in his seat and to be on task, e.g. a behaviour chart (such as shown in Figure 2.3) or personalised monitoring booklet (interventions focused on behaviour, such as shown in Figure 2.4).

If John's reading skills improve and he responds to the reinforcement programme this will hopefully increase his on task behaviour (likely outcome).

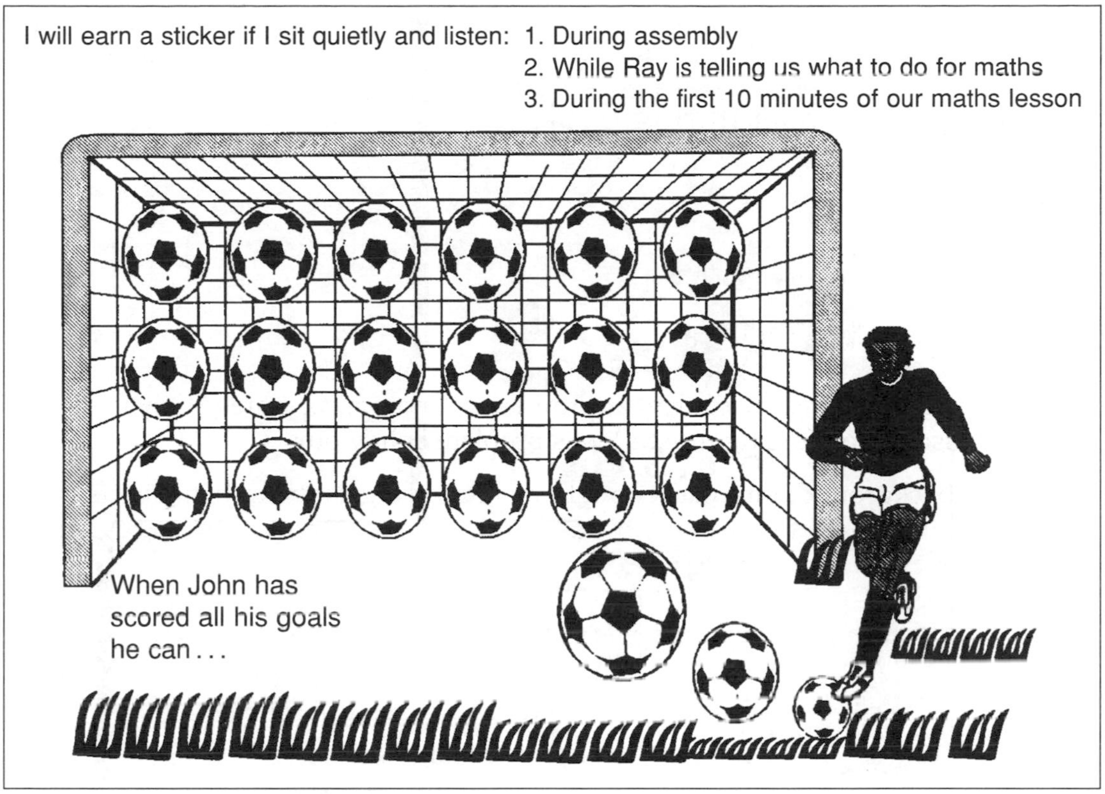

I will earn a sticker if I sit quietly and listen: 1. During assembly
2. While Ray is telling us what to do for maths
3. During the first 10 minutes of our maths lesson

When John has scored all his goals he can...

Figure 2.3 An example of a Behaviour Chart

Behavioural intervention

Definition

A behavioural intervention is a planned, systematic approach to changing behaviour based on classical or operant conditioning. Behavioural interventions can sometimes be combined with interventions based on other perspectives, e.g. the cognitive and biological.

The aim

Behavioural interventions aim to increase appropriate and decrease or extinguish inappropriate behaviours.

The focus

Behavioural interventions can be applied at the individual, group, class or school levels.

The procedure

- Decide on who the participants are, what they will need to do and under what conditions.

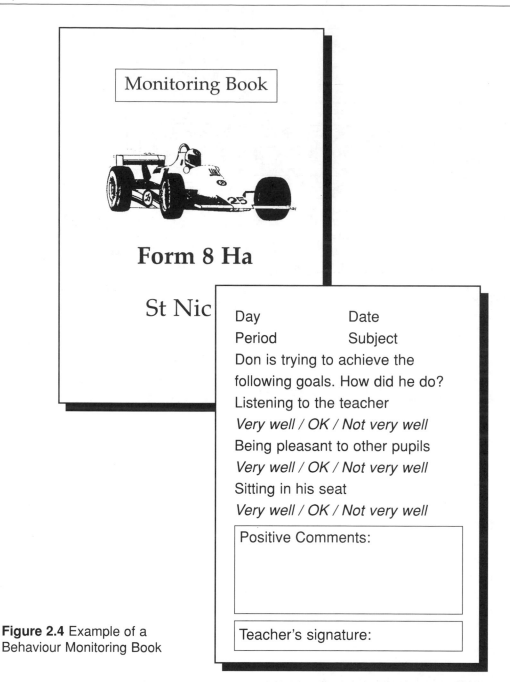

Monitoring Book

Form 8 Ha

St Nic

Day   Date
Period   Subject
Don is trying to achieve the
following goals. How did he do?
Listening to the teacher
Very well / OK / Not very well
Being pleasant to other pupils
Very well / OK / Not very well
Sitting in his seat
Very well / OK / Not very well

Positive Comments:

Teacher's signature:

Figure 2.4 Example of a
Behaviour Monitoring Book

- Decide who the client is: the school, particular teachers, parents or the student.

- Agree on the objectives and targets of the intervention. Targets should be Specific, Measurable, Achievable, Relevant and Time-limited (SMART). Only a few targets should be specified, three or four at the most, and they should be couched where possible in positive terms.

- Establish a pre-intervention baseline to provide a standard for future comparison.

- Establish agreed success criteria or performance indicators that enable teachers and students to agree on what has been achieved in relation to the targets.

- Plan how the intervention will be monitored.

- Plan how the intervention will be phased out.

If the intervention appears to be failing it may be necessary to consider the following points:

- Is reassessment and reformulation indicated?

- Is it necessary to modify or change the intervention?

- Is the student unmotivated or resistant to change?

- Does the student lack the necessary skills and/or resources to cope with the intervention?

- Is the behavioural approach inappropriate for this student?

Types of behavioural interventions

There are basically two types of interventions:
1. those that *increase* appropriate behaviours through:
   - positive reinforcement
   - negative reinforcement
   - shaping
   - contingency contracting
   - token economy

2. those which *decrease* or *terminate* inappropriate behaviours through:
   - extinction
   - time-out
   - punishment
   - response-cost.

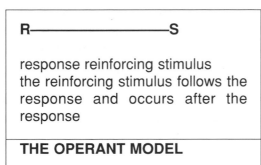

Interventions increasing behaviour

POSITIVE REINFORCEMENT
Positive reinforcement is the immediate presentation of a stimulus following a desired response that increases the likelihood of that response happening again.

R——————————S
response reinforcing stimulus the reinforcing stimulus follows the response and occurs after the response
THE OPERANT MODEL

An example: a teacher praises a student for being on task and the student increases on task behaviour. A positive reinforcer is the reinforcing action.

A positive reinforcer cannot be pre-determined. In order to find out whether something is a reinforcer it is necessary to observe the contingencies between possible reinforcers and behaviours. In other words does the action or event result in an increase in the desired behaviour? This can only be decided empirically. The reason why the reinforcer works and the mental state of the person are both immaterial as all that is needed is an observed increase in the desired behaviour.

The **Premack Principle** (Premack, 1965) states that reinforcement can be seen as a relationship between different probabilities of different types of behaviours. Behaviour of lower probability (the student putting their hand up) is made contingent or conditional on behaviour of higher probability (wanting to play computer games).

In order for reinforcement to be effective the reinforcer must be given immediately after the desired behaviour has been performed.

- *Primary reinforcers* are biologically based, e.g. food and drink. These can be powerful but depend on the student being in a state of deprivation that is unlikely.

- *Secondary reinforcers* are preferable to primary reinforcers. These reinforcers include the use of social reinforcers, e.g. the use of praise, and material reinforcers, e.g. preferred activities, credits, vouchers and tokens. Their value has been learned and unlike primary reinforcers does not have biological significance.

Reinforcers are only considered effective if they bring about an increase in desired behaviour. They can also be affirmative and informative, e.g. praise can indicate that a student's behaviour is 'fine' (affirmative) or 'you have stayed in your seat, well done' (informative). Informative reinforcement is more constructive because it provides feedback to the student.

It should be noted that positive reinforcement could lead to an increase in undesirable behaviour as well as desirable behaviour, e.g. a teacher continually paying immediate attention to a student who calls out all the time.

NEGATIVE REINFORCEMENT

Negative reinforcement is the removal of an aversive stimulus or negative reinforcer that results in a desired behaviour increasing. In the classroom negative reinforcement occurs when a student increases a particular behaviour and as a result the teacher removes something the student does not like. When a student produces more work the teacher stops reprimanding the student.

Negative reinforcement can lead to an increase in undesirable behaviour as well as desirable behaviour. For example, when a student complains about the work, the teacher takes the work away and the student's complaints increase. The student learns that complaining leads to the termination of an aversive stimulus, work.

Using negative reinforcement has disadvantages as it may encourage the student to engage in escape or avoidance behaviours, e.g. the student escaping work by leaving the classroom or avoiding work completely by truanting.

There are various *schedules of reinforcement*, fixed ratio and variable ratio, which are used to vary the rate of delivery of reinforcers. The ratios produce behaviours that are more resistant to extinction by making the required responses more challenging or more unpredictable.

Other types of reinforcement can be tried, for example:

- *differential reinforcement of other behaviour*, where every other behaviour besides the problem behaviour is reinforced;

- *reinforcement of incompatible behaviour*, where behaviour incompatible with the problem behaviour is reinforced;

- *reinforcement of alternative behaviours*, where alternatives to the problem behaviour are reinforced.

SHAPING

Shaping is the consistent reinforcement of successive approximations to the desired behaviour until the desired behaviour is achieved. It is used where the level of performance of the behaviour is infrequent.

During the shaping process the teacher reinforces only those responses that approximate to the desired behaviour. The success criteria shift as the behaviour gets closer to the desired behaviour. An example would be reinforcing small steps that lead a student to acquire a social skill, e.g. co-operating with other students in a small group. Effective shaping requires that:

- clear definition of the target or desired behaviour must be given;

- the student must be performing the behaviour albeit at a low level;

- the intervals must not be too large or too small;

- a decision needs to be made as to how long the student remains at the current level before being encouraged to perform at the next level.

CONTINGENCY CONTRACTING

A behaviour contract is an agreement based on positive reinforcement of target behaviours (example shown in Figure 2.5). It is an agreement between two or more responsible parties that the achievement of specified target behaviours by a student will be positively reinforced. The use of contingency contracting is based on Premack's Principle which states that a behaviour performed at a higher frequency can be used to increase one at a lower frequency or, if you perform x then you will receive y.

The basis of contingency contracting is the individualising of behavioural control so that it reflects the student's needs. The student can play an active role in contracting. Ideally the teacher draws up the contract with the student and with the parents, each party agreeing on their particular roles and responsibilities. Target behaviours should be agreed by all participants and reinforced by the parents as well as the school. For the effective use of contracting certain conditions need to be met:

- reinforcement should be immediate;

- initial contracts should allow for successive approximations;

- reinforcement should be frequent and in small quantities;

- contracts should be couched positively in terms of achievement;

- the contract should be realistic and fair with SMART targets;

- the contract should be clear and unambiguous;

- the contact should not be imposed on the student;

- the contract should be regularly reviewed and evaluated, using success criteria.

TOKEN ECONOMY

A token economy is a reinforcement system in which tokens are earned through a student, group or class performing specific target behaviours. Tokens can take various forms: points, stars, smiling faces, stickers etc. These can be accumulated and used as a means of earning particular rewards, e.g. preferred activities. For a token economy to be effective certain conditions need to be met:

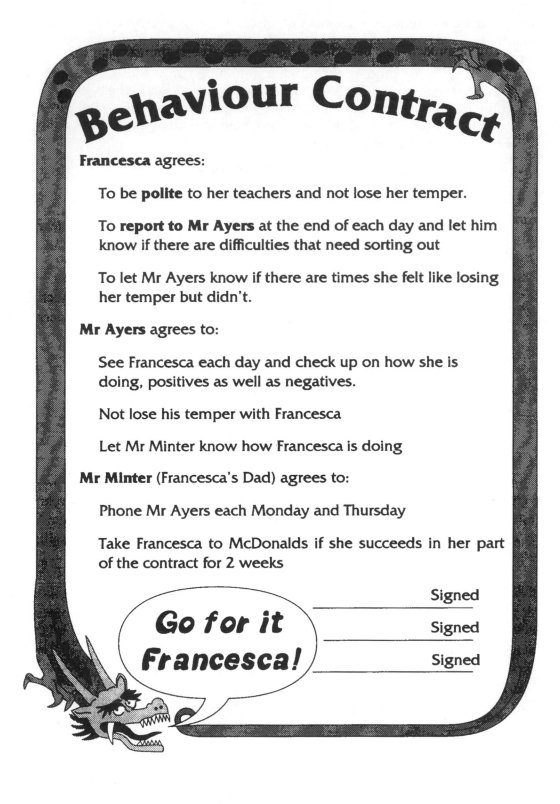

Behaviour Contract

Francesca agrees:

To be **polite** to her teachers and not lose her temper.

To **report to Mr Ayers** at the end of each day and let him know if there are difficulties that need sorting out

To let Mr Ayers know if there are times she felt like losing her temper but didn't.

Mr Ayers agrees to:

See Francesca each day and check up on how she is doing, positives as well as negatives.

Not lose his temper with Francesca

Let Mr Minter know how Francesca is doing

Mr Minter (Francesca's Dad) agrees to:

Phone Mr Ayers each Monday and Thursday

Take Francesca to McDonalds if she succeeds in her part of the contract for 2 weeks

Go for it Francesca!

Signed _____

Signed _____

Signed _____

Figure 2.5 Example of a behaviour contract

- the target behaviours must be clear to students;

- the rate at which tokens are exchanged for rewards must be specified clearly;

- the level of performance required to earn tokens must be established;

- emphasis should be on what students can achieve and earning tokens must be seen as a challenge;

- a reward menu should be agreed and drawn up linking numbers of tokens with rewards;

- initially a limited system should be implemented;

- tokens should be awarded immediately.

Interventions decreasing behaviour

EXTINCTION

The aim of extinction is to withhold or to cease reinforcing a behaviour that has been reinforced, e.g. in the case of a student who keeps demanding and receiving attention by calling out, the teacher stops paying attention and the student stops calling out. For this technique to be effective it has to be:

- based on an observable connection between the teacher's attention and the student's inappropriate behaviour, namely calling out;

- used by the teacher consistently and persistently;

- combined with positive reinforcement of appropriate behaviour;

- based on the consideration as to whether the behaviour can be tolerated until it extinguishes.

TIME-OUT

The idea behind time-out is to remove a student from a situation where the student's problem behaviour is being reinforced to a place that is not reinforcing. A student could be placed in time-out within the classroom or outside the classroom. For time-out to be effective it is necessary to:

- ensure that it is not a rewarding or reinforcing experience;

- ensure that it is consistently used;

- inform the student as to the rule-infringements that will lead to time-out;

- inform the student how time-out will work prior to its use by the teacher.

For a time-out room or area to be effective the following conditions should be met:

- the room should not reinforce the student's behaviour, e.g. being able to chat and laugh with other students and avoid class work;

- the time spent in the room should be as brief as possible;

- the room should be adequately supervised;

- records should be kept by teachers detailing the student's punctuality, attendance and behaviour while in the room, the reasons for being sent there and the teachers who referred the student to the room.

PUNISHMENT

The aim of punishment is to decrease or terminate problem behaviours through the application of an aversive stimulus. There are two types: the use of an aversive stimulus as a result of the specific behaviour, e.g. a reprimand, detention and writing out of lines, or alternatively taking away from students something that they like, e.g. a privilege; this is called response-cost. Punishment in these senses in the short term is undoubtedly effective but its use over a long period can lead to problems:

- it may simply suppress the student's behaviour temporarily;

- it presents a negative way of relating to others for the student to model, e.g. aggression;

- it does not inform the student precisely, as to which specific behaviour should be performed;

- it can lead to the student experiencing emotional stress, becoming withdrawn or avoiding the lesson;

- it may evoke in the student intense dislike of the person who punishes rather than change the student's behaviour;

- what the teacher perceives as punishment may actually be reinforcing for the student, e.g. being sent out of the class.

If punishment is used then it is better to implement it in the following ways:

- specify for which rule-infringements punishment will be used and draw up a graded tariff of punishments;

- display in the classroom a code of conduct;

- apply the punishment consistently and immediately;

- apply the punishment fairly to all offending students;

- avoid punishing a group or class for the misbehaviour of a student or students;

- avoid being emotional when punishing students;

- use positive reinforcement as well as punishment.

With regard to reprimands it is better to:

- use them in relation to specific behaviour;

- avoid using them to be derogatory towards the student;

- use them immediately along with loss of privileges;

- avoid sarcasm or embarrassing the student in front of others;

- avoid referring to or harping on past incidents;

- try and use non-verbal reprimands along with or instead of verbal reprimands.

Behavioural evaluation

This type of evaluation is dependent on establishing a pre-intervention baseline that means determining systematically the frequency and duration of the observable target behaviours of an identified student over a number of weeks. This is achieved by using appropriate observation schedules. This baseline will be a benchmark for comparing the frequency and duration of the target behaviours after an intervention.

By making comparisons between the pre-intervention baseline and the end point of the intervention it should be possible to evaluate the intervention through observing that the target behaviours have either increased or decreased or that no change had occurred. This can provide an objective account of changes in a student's behaviour given the caveats of observer reactivity and bias. This structured approach is to be contrasted with the subjectivity of a teacher's perception based on perhaps erratic and intermittent observation of a student's behaviour.

Experimental designs are employed to tease out those factors that are believed to influence changes in behaviour. The fact that behaviour has improved does not necessarily mean that the intervention used has brought about improvement. Behavioural change may have been brought about by factors external or coincidental with the changes in behaviour. In other words correlation does necessarily equal causation.

The main experimental designs are *reversal* and *multiple-baseline designs*. The reversal design (ABAB) is where the original baseline A, is followed by B, an intervention, then a return to the original baseline A through withdrawing the intervention. Then the intervention B is reintroduced. If behaviour improves through B and then returns to its original state A after the withdrawal of the intervention and then improves after being reintroduced again then it is assumed that the intervention is responsible for the improvement.

In the multiple-baseline design the same intervention is directed at a number of behaviours, e.g. across different students. The intervention is used first with one student then with the others in succession. If the intervention is responsible for behavioural improvement then one would expect to see change in each student's behaviour following immediately on the intervention.

The behavioural approach to teaching and learning

This approach advocated by Wheldall *et al.* (1986) is outlined below.

Basic assumptions

- It is a structured approach that leads to appropriate practice.

- This approach has been found to be effective empirically in many different institutional, interpersonal and personal contexts.

- Most behaviour is learned within the limits set by genetics and is the result of an interaction between the individual and their environment. Behaviour is shaped through reinforcing events.

- Behaviour is relative to what is considered adaptive or maladaptive in a given social or cultural context.

- Many emotional and behavioural problems are the result of faulty learning or failure to learn, i.e. they arise through the processes of classical and operant conditioning.

- Cognitive and unconscious processes are not included in this approach except in the case of the cognitive-behavioural perspective where consideration of cognitive processes is integrated with the behavioural approach.

- This approach is seen as desirable in terms of it being easy to learn, easy to implement and amenable to empirical evaluation.

Techniques

This approach refers to the application of behavioural techniques to teaching and refers to the theory that behaviour is primarily the result of learning but that what is learnt can be changed. Behavioural change can be achieved by controlling the consequences of that behaviour. The main teaching points are:

- Teachers should direct their attention to their students' observable behaviour in the classroom and overt and observable factors that influence that behaviour. This is preferable to speculating about unconscious conflicts or underlying problems that arise during early infancy as such speculation is based on a high level of inference. Teachers should carefully define and observe the specific and overt problem behaviour of their students and base their judgements on these definitions and observations.

- Nearly all student pupil behaviour is the result of learning. Genetics sets limits but behaviour is still the result of learning within those limits. Positive and negative behaviour can be learned but can also be unlearned. Teachers need to think of strategies that encourage their pupils to learn appropriate behaviour or unlearn inappropriate behaviour.

- Behavioural change needs to be measured. Measurement enables teachers to be more precise and objective in estimating how far pupils have improved their behaviour. This measurement is achieved through a frequency count of the pupil's problem behaviours and by referring to latency, duration and severity.

- Pupils learn on the basis of repeating behaviours that have been reinforced or rewarded. The emphasis should be on the teacher rewarding students for positive behaviour and setting up situations which students find rewarding or where they can be rewarded. There is evidence supporting the idea that rewarding positive behaviour is more effective than punishment.

- Behaviour is also influenced by its context or environment, therefore it is necessary for the teacher to consider the effects of their classroom environment on their students' behaviour in terms of reinforcement. The context refers to not only the classroom itself but also aspects like seating or grouping arrangements.

3 The cognitive-behavioural perspective

The cognitive model

The cognitive-behavioural perspective developed in response to the limitations of the purely behavioural model. The same stimulus produced different responses in different people. This suggested the influence of cognitive processes, i.e. thinking and reasoning. The bases of this perspective are:

- cognitive processes are associated with behaviours;
- cognitive processes can bring about changes in behaviour;
- cognitive processes can be assessed, changed and evaluated.

Cognitive processes include perceptions, attitudes, images, expectations, attributions and beliefs. Given that these processes lead to the performance of certain kinds of behaviour, changing these processes should lead to changes in behaviour. For example, students' thinking and reasoning processes are influential in how they will respond to teachers and situations. They may respond differently to the same situations or the same teachers depending on their attitudes and assumptions. Cognitive approaches are combined with behavioural approaches to form the cognitive-behavioural perspective. It should be noted that the results of the cognitive approach could be open to alternative explanations, e.g. as causes, consequences or correlation. This perspective has been applied to a wide range of mild to severe emotional and behavioural disorders.

In bringing about changes in problem behaviour it is necessary to consider the influence of a student's thinking and reasoning on those behaviours. There are a number of cognitive approaches that address problem behaviours. These include Rational Emotive Behavioural Therapy (A. Ellis), Cognitive Therapy (A. Beck), Self-control Theory (M. Rosenbaum), Self-instructional Training (D. Meichenbaum), Problem-solving Skills Training (T.J. D'Zurilla and M.R. Goldfried), Stress-inoculation Training (D. Meichenbaum) and Attribution Retraining (A. Bandura and M.L. Weiner).

Evaluation of the cognitive perspective

The cognitive perspective is often combined with the behavioural perspective to form the cognitive-behavioural perspective. It refers to mental events that are associated with or that influence behaviour; these events are excluded from the behavioural perspective. The cognitive perspective enlarges therefore the number of factors that are seen to control or influence behaviour. This perspective in the form of cognitive-behavioural therapies and interventions has a wide application for treating not only mild or moderate emotional and behavioural problems but also severe mental disorders, e.g. psychoses.

This perspective refers to non-observable cognitive events and from the behavioural perspective these are regarded as unscientific concepts. The cognitive approach does not refer to unconscious or psychodynamic processes. Rather it refers to conscious awareness or cognitive appraisal and current thinking and reasoning. Subjective experience is seen as a process that can be accessed and assessed. Finally it might be argued that changes in cognitions are the result of changes in feeling and behaviour rather than the causes of those changes.

Cognitive assessment

Cognitive assessment is a type of assessment that examines cognitive processes and how they relate or connect to problem behaviours. It is an attempt to identify the specific patterns of thoughts, thinking and reasoning processes individual students engage in and the consequences for their behaviour. Through identifying cognitive processes it is hoped that behavioural change can be facilitated.

The methods of cognitive assessment include the following techniques: self-report, interviews, behaviour rating scales, direction observation and sociometry. These techniques provide results that can be used to assess self-concept, task performance, attitudes towards others, locus of control and attribution style.

Self-reports

Students can complete accurate reports on their attitudes towards tasks, teachers and other students as well as about their own feelings and self-esteem. They can also report on their *perceived self-efficacy* and *attributions*. This means that students can be placed on self-report in order to assess their expectations of success in performing desirable behaviours. They can also be assessed in terms of their attributional styles. A student's *attributional style* is the way in which a student makes similar attribution of causes across different times and contexts. Attributional style is based on three dimensions: *internal-external*, *global-specific* and *stable-unstable*. Students who have an internal, global and stable style are likely to blame themselves, to see their problems as applying to all contexts and as permanent. These students tend to be unmotivated. Students may have an *internal* or *external locus of control* (Rotter, 1966). It is internal if students see the causes of their behaviours as being under their control, external if outside their control. Students having an internal locus of control are more likely to improve their behaviour.

Interviews

In interviews students can describe the thoughts that are associated with their problem behaviour, e.g. other students, teachers and contexts.

Interviewing parents

Parents should be asked their thoughts about their son or daughter's problem behaviours along with their developmental and behavioural histories.

Interviewing students

- Find out the students' level of awareness of the problem behaviour.
- Find out the students' accounts of the problems they experience and their attributional style, i.e. whether they blame themselves or others for their problems.
- Find out whether the student lacks problem-solving skills.
- Find out student's expectations and awareness of others' expectations.
- Find out whether the student lacks motivation and attitudes towards rewards and punishments.

The Cognitive Assessment Pupil Questionnaire (shown in Figure 3.1 and in full in the resources section at the back of the book) can be used to record a student's perceptions of their behaviour in the classroom and around the school.

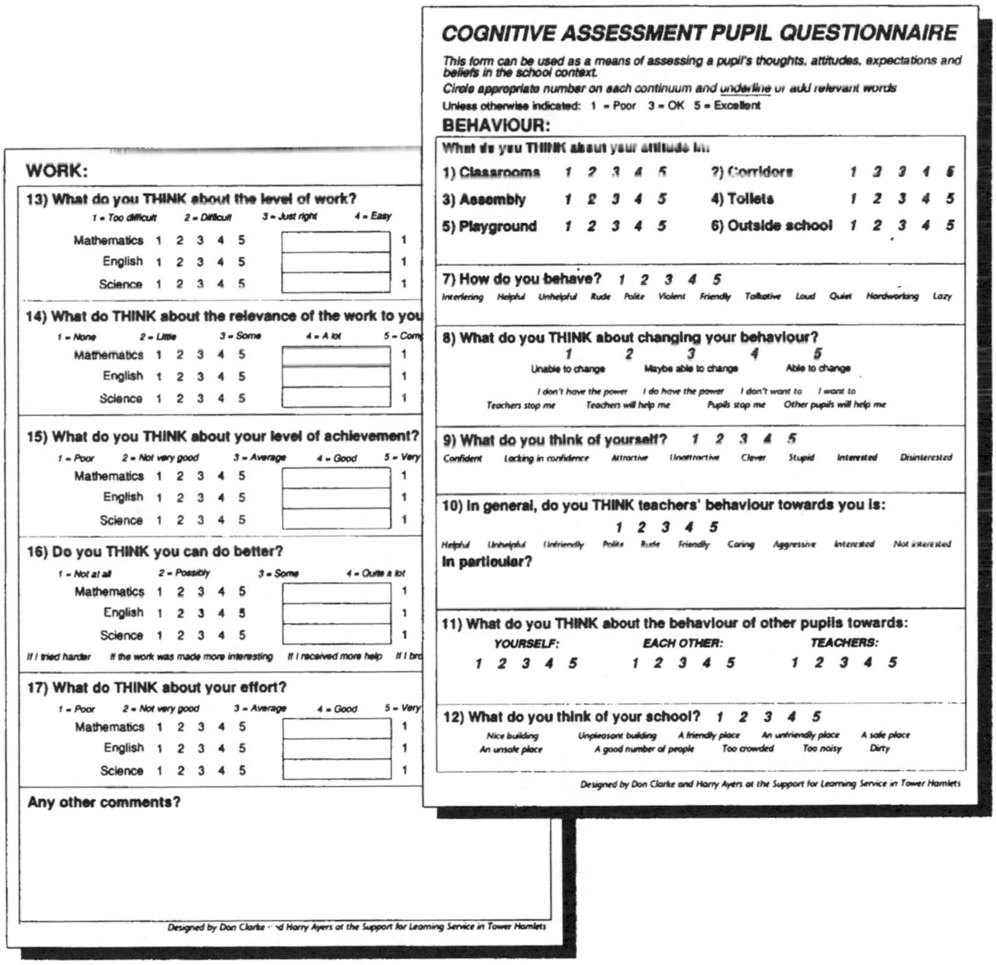

COGNITIVE ASSESSMENT PUPIL QUESTIONNAIRE

This form can be used as a means of assessing a pupil's thoughts, attitudes, expectations and beliefs in the school context.

Circle appropriate number on each continuum and underline or add relevant words

Unless otherwise indicated: 1 = Poor 3 = OK 5 = Excellent

BEHAVIOUR:

What do you THINK about your attitude in:

1) Classrooms 1 2 3 4 5 2) Corridors 1 2 3 4 5
3) Assembly 1 2 3 4 5 4) Toilets 1 2 3 4 5
5) Playground 1 2 3 4 5 6) Outside school 1 2 3 4 5

7) How do you behave? 1 2 3 4 5
Interfering Helpful Unhelpful Rude Polite Violent Friendly Talkative Loud Quiet Hardworking Lazy

8) What do you THINK about changing your behaviour?
1 2 3 4 5
Unable to change Maybe able to change Able to change
I don't have the power I do have the power I don't want to I want to
Teachers stop me Teachers will help me Pupils stop me Other pupils will help me

9) What do you think of yourself? 1 2 3 4 5
Confident Lacking in confidence Attractive Unattractive Clever Stupid Interested Disinterested

10) In general, do you THINK teachers' behaviour towards you is:
1 2 3 4 5
Helpful Unhelpful Unfriendly Polite Rude Friendly Caring Aggressive Interested Not interested
In particular?

11) What do you THINK about the behaviour of other pupils towards:
YOURSELF: 1 2 3 4 5 EACH OTHER: 1 2 3 4 5 TEACHERS: 1 2 3 4 5

12) What do you think of your school? 1 2 3 4 5
Nice building Unpleasant building A friendly place An unfriendly place A safe place
An unsafe place A good number of people Too crowded Too noisy Dirty

Designed by Don Clarke and Harry Ayers at the Support for Learning Service in Tower Hamlets

WORK:

13) What do you THINK about the level of work?
1 = Too difficult 2 = Difficult 3 = Just right 4 = Easy
Mathematics 1 2 3 4 5
English 1 2 3 4 5
Science 1 2 3 4 5

14) What do THINK about the relevance of the work to you
1 = None 2 = Little 3 = Some 4 = A lot 5 = Com
Mathematics 1 2 3 4 5
English 1 2 3 4 5
Science 1 2 3 4 5

15) What do you THINK about your level of achievement?
1 = Poor 2 = Not very good 3 = Average 4 = Good 5 = Very
Mathematics 1 2 3 4 5
English 1 2 3 4 5
Science 1 2 3 4 5

16) Do you THINK you can do better?
1 = Not at all 2 = Possibly 3 = Some 4 = Quite a lot
Mathematics 1 2 3 4 5
English 1 2 3 4 5
Science 1 2 3 4 5
If I tried harder If the work was made more interesting If I received more help If I br

17) What do THINK about your effort?
1 = Poor 2 = Not very good 3 = Average 4 = Good 5 = Very
Mathematics 1 2 3 4 5
English 1 2 3 4 5
Science 1 2 3 4 5

Any other comments?

Designed by Don Clarke and Harry Ayers at the Support for Learning Service in Tower Hamlets

Figure 3.1 The Cognitive Assessment Pupil Questionnaire

Interviewing teachers

- Find out if and in what ways the teacher thinks the student is a problem.
- Find out the teacher's expectations of the student.
- Find out whether the teacher thinks the student lacks problem-solving skills.

Behaviour rating scales

These scales enable teachers to rate a student's behaviours according to their perceptions of those behaviours. They are useful in providing ratings from a number of teachers, enabling comparisons of ratings between teachers. (See Figures 3.2 and 3.3 which shows the Primary and Secondary Assessment Profiles. These enable teachers to record their perceptions of students' behaviours under 20 categories.)

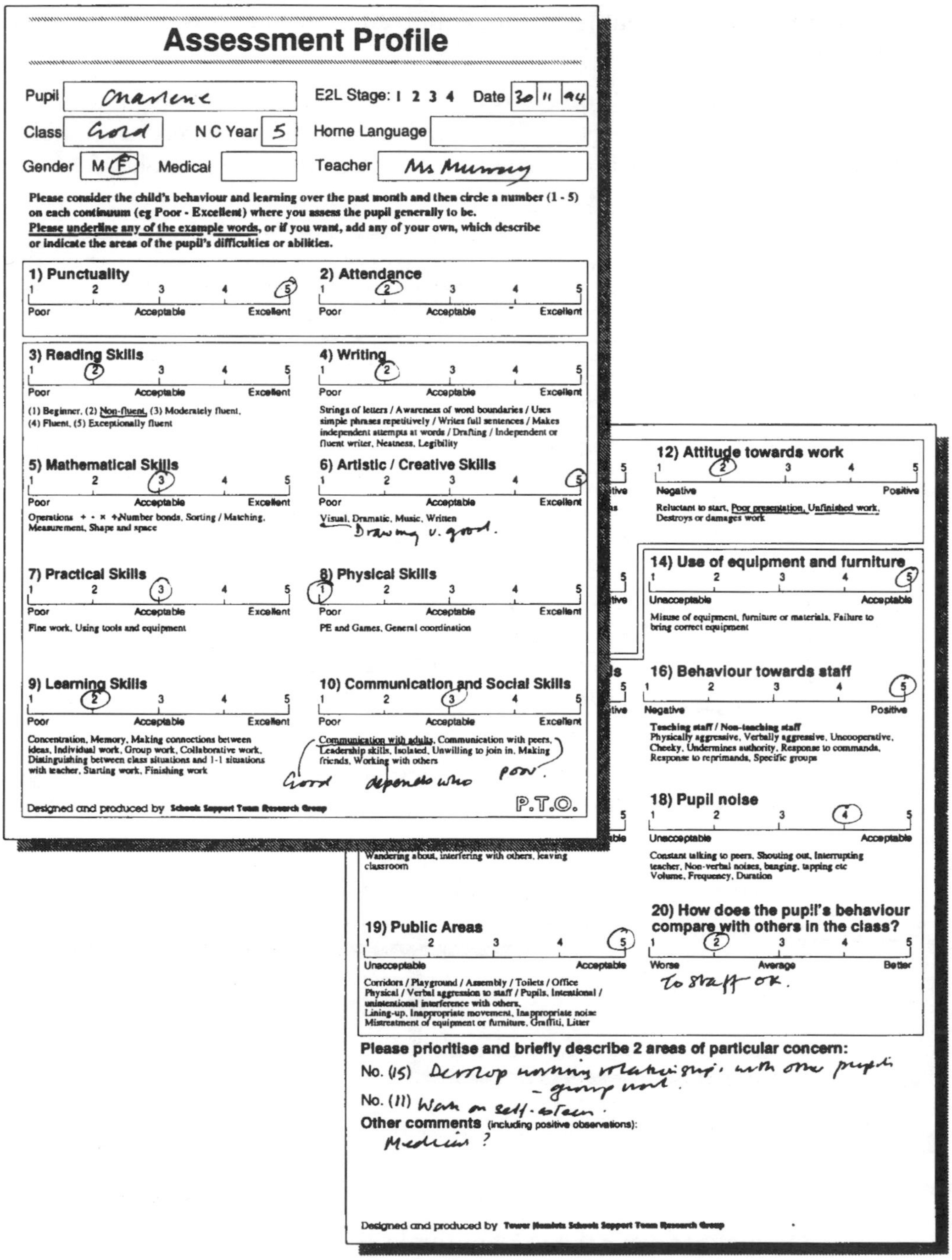

Figure 3.2 The Assessment Profile from Assessing Individual Needs

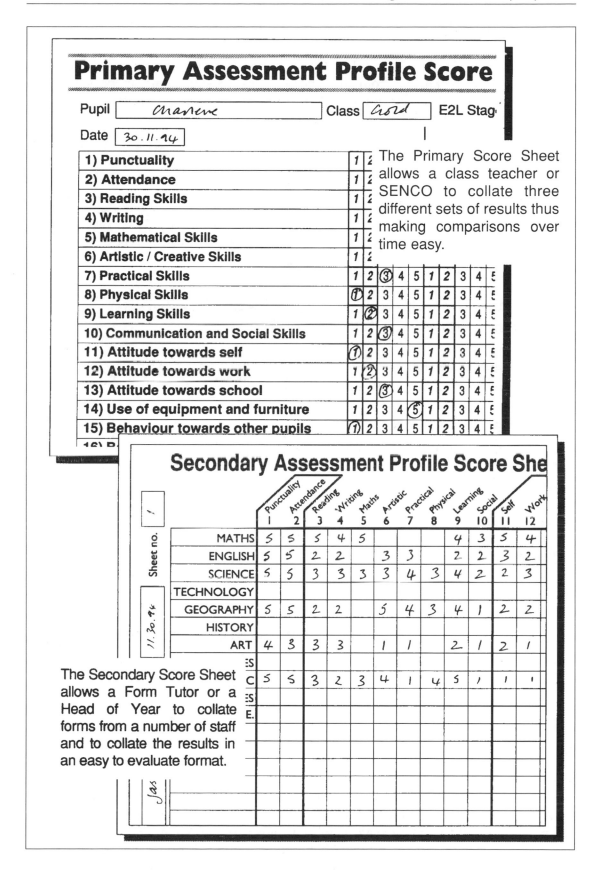

Primary Assessment Profile Score

Pupil: Chanere Class: Gold E2L Stage

Date: 30.11.94

1) Punctuality	1	2	
2) Attendance	1	2	
3) Reading Skills	1	2	
4) Writing	1	2	
5) Mathematical Skills	1	2	
6) Artistic / Creative Skills	1	2	
7) Practical Skills	1 2 ③ 4 5	1 2 3 4 5	
8) Physical Skills	① 2 3 4 5	1 2 3 4 5	
9) Learning Skills	1 ② 3 4 5	1 2 3 4 5	
10) Communication and Social Skills	1 2 ③ 4 5	1 2 3 4 5	
11) Attitude towards self	① 2 3 4 5	1 2 3 4 5	
12) Attitude towards work	1 ② 3 4 5	1 2 3 4 5	
13) Attitude towards school	1 2 ③ 4 5	1 2 3 4 5	
14) Use of equipment and furniture	1 2 3 4 ⑤	1 2 3 4 5	
15) Behaviour towards other pupils	① 2 3 4 5	1 2 3 4 5	
16) B...			

The Primary Score Sheet allows a class teacher or SENCO to collate three different sets of results thus making comparisons over time easy.

Secondary Assessment Profile Score She

Sheet no.

11.30.94

	Punctuality 1	Attendance 2	Reading 3	Writing 4	Maths 5	Artistic 6	Practical 7	Physical 8	Learning 9	Social 10	Self 11	Work 12
MATHS	5	5	5	4	5				4	3	5	4
ENGLISH	5	5	2	2		3	3		2	2	3	2
SCIENCE	5	5	3	3	3	3	4	3	4	2	2	3
TECHNOLOGY												
GEOGRAPHY	5	5	2	2		5	4	3	4	1	2	2
HISTORY												
ART	4	3	3	3		1	1		2	1	2	1
ES												
C	5	5	3	2	3	4	1	4	5	1	1	1
ES												
E.												

The Secondary Score Sheet allows a Form Tutor or a Head of Year to collate forms from a number of staff and to collate the results in an easy to evaluate format.

Figure 3.3

Direct observation

Behavioural observation is useful in that it is possible to infer students' thoughts, attitudes and expectations from their behaviours. Observation can be structured through the use of Fixed Interval Sampling, Behaviour Frequency, Cognitive Monitoring (see Figure 3.4) and ABC sheets.

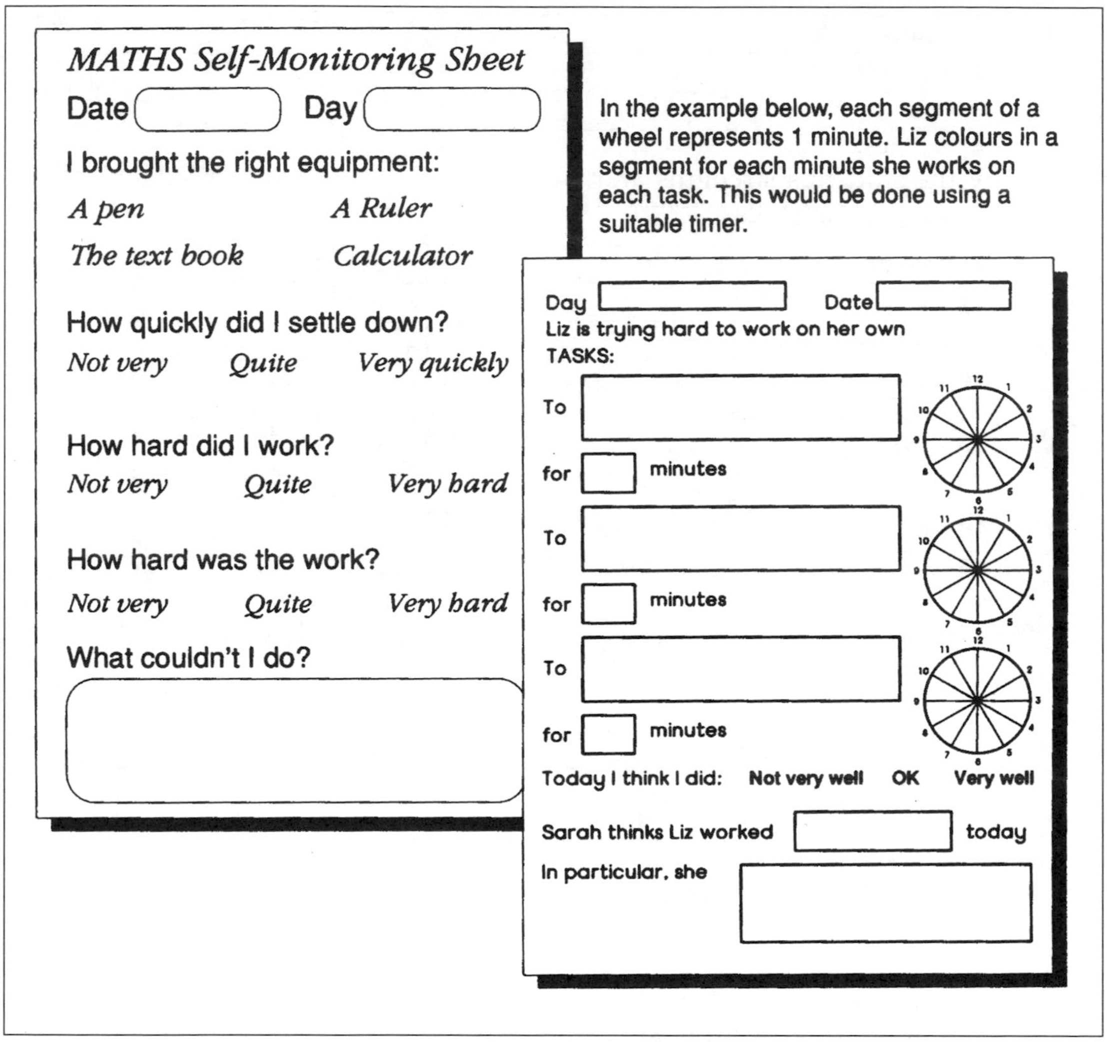

Figure 3.4 Example of pages from cognitive monitoring books

Sociometry

This form of assessment provides information on the opinions and attitudes towards other students. It provides a guide to students' degree of acceptance of other students, and whether students are rejected or isolated. Students can be asked with whom they would work or play or whom they like or dislike. Finally they can be asked to describe the personality and behaviour of other students. The results can be illustrated in a sociogram. The sociogram can be used in an intervention directed at reintegrating students into peer groups.

The assessment procedure

After selecting from the above methods of assessment it is advisable to proceed through the following procedure:

- Identify the student's behaviour problems and associated thinking and reasoning processes in consultation with staff, parents, carers and the student.

- Identify the student's attributional style, perceived level of self-efficacy and whether the student has an internal or external locus of control.

- Find out the contexts, frequency, duration and intensity of the student's behavioural problems.

- Identify the student's strengths and weaknesses with regard to problem-solving and communication skills.

- Decide through motivational interviewing whether the student possesses the motivation to change.

- Arrive at a formulation based on the assessment.

Cognitive formulation

Cognitive assessments should lead directly to cognitive formulations which are based on hypotheses that relate students' thinking and reasoning processes to their problem behaviours. A cognitive formulation should combine the following elements:

- brief and specific descriptions of students' problem behaviours and associated patterns of thinking and reasoning;

- the attributional style, locus of control, perceived level of self efficacy and motivational level of the students and the influence they have on students' problem behaviours;

- those cognitive factors that serve to maintain the students' problem behaviours.

Example: a NCY 7 boy

Description

The boy refuses to answer questions from a class textbook when asked by the History teacher and becomes rude to the teacher if pressed. He has had reading difficulties from an early age and suffers from low self-esteem.

Reasons – internal

The boy attributes his failure to read adequately to a lack of ability and feels that this lack is fixed and unalterable. He has an internal attributional style that is self-defeating in that it discourages him from attempting to make any effort to improve his reading skills.

Reasons – external

There is parental criticism due to his lack of progress in reading at school and unfavourable comparisons with his sister who reads well. They too attribute his failure to lack of ability.

Maintaining factors

His reading problems and the associated negative thoughts lead him to want to avoid future failure. He anticipates and expects failure. He avoids embarrassment and shame by refusing to read and by refusing to answer questions. This compounds the problem generating a low level of self-efficacy. This is intensified by parental criticism of his perceived ability and by comparisons to his sister.

The teacher confirms his feelings of failure by asking him to read a textbook that is too difficult. His peers taunt him over his reading difficulty and this leads him to want to avoid school altogether. He feels embarrassed in front of his peers as he compares himself unfavourably to them. All this confirms his internal attribution, that is, seeing himself as 'thick' and therefore unable to improve his reading skills. Therefore he makes no effort to do so and all around him parents, teacher and his peers attribute his failure to his perceived lack of ability. This formulation should lead to particular interventions:

- Changing the attributional style of not only the student, but also the teacher and the parents through psychological assessment. This assessment could indicate that his reading difficulty is remediable and could be addressed through peer tutoring in school and paired reading at home. These methods could serve two aims, i.e. to increase his reading skills and help shift the parents and peers towards more positive attributions.

- Increasing his perceived self-efficacy and self-esteem by recognising and acknowledging his particular strengths in Art, Drama and Technology.

- Differentiating the work set for the student. The teacher could provide a differentiated worksheet or approach that enabled the student to experience some success with the task and answer some of the teacher's questions.

Cognitive interventions

General

There is a range of cognitive interventions or therapies. The use of particular interventions and therapies depends on an assessment of the student in terms of the level of cognitive development, their cognitive strengths and weaknesses attained rather than simply their chronological ages. The focus of cognitive intervention is on changing or modifying students' cognitions (beliefs, attitudes, expectations, attributions and perceived self-efficacy) that in turn lead to behavioural changes.

Cognitive therapies

Rational Emotive Behaviour Therapy (REBT)

Albert Ellis founded this form of cognitive-behavioural therapy. This approach is based on the idea that people have a biological predisposition to hold certain beliefs about themselves, others and the external environment. These beliefs are seen as influencing feelings and behaviours. Some beliefs will lead to positive and other beliefs to negative feelings and behaviours. It is possible to modify or change the negative feeling and behaviour. Basically people disturb themselves by their thinking. There are two types of beliefs, rational and irrational. Rational beliefs are positive and self-enhancing whereas irrational beliefs are negative and self-defeating.

Irrational beliefs are absolutistic and demanding expressed in terms of 'ought to', 'have to' and 'must have'. These beliefs are also inconsistent with reality and illogical. Irrational beliefs lead to emotional and behavioural problems, e.g. depression and social isolation.

There are different types of irrational beliefs that result in unrealistic or unqualified expectations of others, e.g.

- blaming and damning others when they are unfair;

- viewing everything as hopeless, awful and catastrophic;

- everything that happens is outside one's control;

- it is easier to avoid rather than deal with problems;

- the past determines the present, everything will continue as it has done in the past.

Many types of irrational beliefs appear to derive from hasty over-generalisations.

Ellis developed an *ABC model* in which emotional and behavioural consequences (C) are influenced by a person's cognitive processes, e.g. rational or irrational beliefs (B) regarding particular activating events (A) (see Figure 3.4).

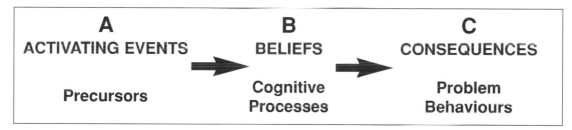

Figure 3.5 ABC model (Ellis)

The aim of REBT is to identify and challenge or dispute current irrational thinking that leads to emotional and behavioural problems. Thus the focus and emphasis is on the here and now rather than the past. It disputes those beliefs from an empirical and logical standpoint. Are they consistent with reality and logic? The aim would be to test students' beliefs, i.e. the empirical or logical bases of students' beliefs. These are beliefs about themselves, others and the world. This approach also looks at the pragmatic results or consequences of holding irrational beliefs.

Students may think that all teachers or all their peers should like them or that everybody is against them. They may think that they have to achieve top marks in all subjects. The aims of the intervention would be to dispute these generalisations, for example by pointing out exceptions and by showing the negative consequences for the students of believing these generalisations.

Cognitive therapy (CT)

Aaron Beck developed cognitive therapy. It is based on the *phenomenological* and *information-processing* approaches to thinking and behaviour. It studies the way people construct their experiences, including people's perceptions and interpretations of those experiences. There are voluntary thoughts that are directly accessible and automatic thoughts. *Automatic thoughts* are difficult to access and if persistent may lead to emotional problems. Finally there are *schemas*, organising principles that influence people's views of themselves, others and the external world. Schemas are a set of core beliefs established in infancy that are triggered by particular events. They can be narrow or broad, flexible or rigid. When schemas are activated negative automatic thoughts can arise along with distortions in the way information is processed. *Cognitive distortions* are biases in the selection and assimilation of behaviour. They reinforce schemas. Schemas when activated also generate *cognitive deficits*, e.g. difficulties with perception, inference, retention and recall.

Behavioural change is partly achieved through examining or testing the empirical bases of people's beliefs. This process is called *collaborative empiricism* when counsellors and clients work together to test their beliefs empirically. Additionally, people are encouraged to generate alternative interpretations and explanations that will lead to changes in their behaviour. The focus is on people's beliefs about self, perceived self-efficacy, attributions, predictions and attitudes towards other people and the external world. Common *cognitive deficits* or errors are:

- *arbitrary inference* – jumping to conclusions;

- *selective abstraction* – focusing on one thing to the exclusion of others;

- *over-generalisation* – generalising from the particular to the general without good reason or evidence;

- *magnification and minimisation* – attributing too much or too little significance to events;

- *personalisation* – relating events or incidents to oneself when there is no real connection;

- *dichotomous thinking* – dividing one's thinking or experience into either-or categories.

The individual examines their thinking or experience for the presence of cognitive errors and after identifying them they are in a position to rectify them. This requires self-monitoring.

Cognitive therapy encourages people to monitor automatic thoughts, to recognise relationships between thoughts, feelings and behaviour, to replace unrealistic with realistic thoughts and to change core beliefs that generate emotional and behavioural problems.

Example: Beck's cognitive theory of depression

Beck's theory is that people experience depression though activation of a latent *depressogenic schema*. The activation of this schema leads to symptoms of depression, e.g. sadness, hopelessness, passivity and social withdrawal. In terms of information processing, positive information is filtered out and negative information is selected and assimilated. The depressogenic schema is not the cause of depression but a way in which a depression proliferates. The activation of the schema leads to cognitive deficits (e.g. memory problems) and cognitive distortions (e.g. selective abstraction and personalisation). The schema generates a *cognitive triad*: negative views of the self (as failing), the world (as hostile) and the future (as hopeless). Hopelessness is seen by Beck as a key factor in suicidal ideation.

BECK'S THREE-COLUMN TECHNIQUE

This technique as shown in Figure 3.6 is used to display examples of the cognitive errors made by students. Teachers can undertake cognitive interventions based on REBT and CT. They can identify, challenge and modify the irrational ideas and cognitive errors of their students through logical and empirical methods.

Situation/context	Thoughts/beliefs	Logical errors
A teacher dislikes me	All teachers dislike me	Over-generalisation
Waiting for test result	I was the last to finish, I must have failed	Arbitrary inference
	The teacher did not smile at me, I must have failed	Personalisation
	Even if I fail it doesn't matter	Minimisation

Figure 3.6

Cognitive-mediation and coping skills approaches

Self-management or self-control training (M. Rosenbaum)

This approach focuses on the use of language to control behaviour. The emphasis is on identifying students' language skills and their internal dialogues. This approach requires self-recording of students' thoughts through self-observation and self-monitoring. Thoughts, beliefs and feelings are identified and recorded. Self-evaluation enables students to compare their standards of behaviour, past and present.

Rosenbaum's theory (1990, 1993) outlines three types of self-control: *redressive*, *reformative* and *experiential*. Redressive self-control focuses on students regulating and maintaining target behaviours even when challenged through, for example, positive self-talk. Reformative self-control focuses on students changing their current behaviours and performing new behaviours through, for example, action planning and problem-solving. Experiential self-control focuses on students developing self-awareness particular with regard to their feelings and external stimuli. Through developing self-awareness students open themselves up to new experiences and learn new skills.

Self-instructional training (D. Meichenbaum)

This approach suggests that the development of self-control involves a gradual change from external to self-control through the internalisation of instructions. It is based on the work of Vygotsky (1962). Meichenbaum and Goodman (1971) developed a programme for treating impulsive behaviour. The aims were to train students in the use of verbal self-instructions, appropriate responses and self-reinforcement. The stages in the intervention are as follows:

- modelling of the appropriate behaviour with overt instructions;
- student imitates the behaviour along with overt self-instruction;
- student imitates and whispers self-instruction;
- pupil imitates with covert self-instruction.

Generally intervention takes the form of teaching the skills related to self-instruction:

- defining the problem behaviour;

- looking at the approach to the problem;

- looking at how to focus on the problem;

- using coping statements for changing problem behaviours;

- developing the process of self-reinforcement for appropriate behaviour.

Problem-solving skills training (T.J. D'Zurilla and M.R. Goldfried)

D'Zurilla's (1986) problem-solving approach is based on a five-stage model that aims to equip students with problem-solving skills. The five stages are:

- orientation;

- problem definition and formulation;

- positing alternatives;

- decision-making;

- verification.

This approach involves training students in specific problem-solving skills. These skills are listed as follows:

- preventing initial impulsive responses – stopping and thinking;

- identifying problems – ways of recognising problems;

- generating alternatives – brainstorming;

- thinking about the consequences of pursuing certain actions;

- planning a solution;

- evaluating the plan.

This type of problem-solving intervention has been used with students who are impulsive and disruptive. It is also an intervention that can be used with students who experience interpersonal problems. The underlying assumption is that students with behavioural problems lack the cognitive skills that are essential for positive social interactions between teachers and students. Disruptive and aggressive students are seen as in need of developing alternative ways of thinking and behaving. Their goals may be acceptable but the means or strategies to achieve those goals, inappropriate.

Teachers in collaboration with students can devise behaviour plans. These are problem-solving plans that students are able to put into practice. Bill Rogers' Behaviour Recovery is a good example. A behaviour plan may take the following form. The teacher with the student:

- identifies and clarifies the problems and the target behaviours; they both agree that the student wants to receive positive attention from other students and that he attempts unsuccessfully to obtain this through making aggressive demands; the target behaviours should consist of non-aggressive actions that gain positive attention;

- consider alternative ways of coping with the problem, e.g. both agree that the student should offer to help or share something with the other students;

- outline the steps required to achieve the appropriate behaviour, e.g. arrange for the students concerned to be a part of his group and for those students to be prepared to accept him into their group;

- discuss the possible consequences of behaving in certain ways, e.g. offering help or sharing is more likely to gain positive attention from the other students whereas aggression is more likely to alienate and antagonise them as it will lead to the student being rejected and feeling even more frustrated and angry, especially as the goal will not have been successfully achieved.

Stress-inoculation training (D. Meichenbaum)

Meichenbaum emphasises the importance of acquiring coping skills that enable students to deal with small, manageable amounts of stress as a means of resolving larger problems. Once students can tolerate small amounts of stress then it is assumed that they will be able to cope with increased amounts and also feel they have greater self-control.

THREE-STAGE MODEL PROPOSED BY MEICHENBAUM AND CAMERON (1973)

- didactic or direct instruction as to the nature of stress;

- teaching coping skills, e.g. relaxation techniques, use of positive self-statements and self-reinforcement;

- exposure to stressful events that enables the student to practise their newly acquired coping skills, called behaviour rehearsal.

This approach has been used for anger-management. The emphasis is on students self-monitoring their anger behaviour and the events and thoughts preceding their anger. For this purpose students are provided with self-control monitoring forms that enable them to record their thoughts, feelings and behaviour in particular situations when they lose self-control and become angry. This enables students to reflect on their anger problems and puts them in a better position to control their anger.

Attribution retraining (A. Bandura and M.L. Weiner)

This approach emphasises how students' causal explanations and attributions influence their problem behaviour in the present and in the future. Students' attributions can be based on a number of cognitive processing errors. For example, students overestimate the likelihood of negative events (e.g. unfair treatment or hostile intent) and misattribute or jump to conclusions in ambiguous situations (e.g. glances or looks are always interpreted as hostile). When students make incorrect attributions about the causes of their problems these attributions can adversely affect their behaviour. Students may see their problems as always caused by other students or by their teachers and assume no responsibility for their problems. Where students accept responsibility they may claim they have no control over their behaviour.

Attribution retraining is directed at encouraging students to identify their attributions, particularly errors in thinking and reasoning. Students are asked to contemplate alternatives and to put them into practice in different contexts. The aim is to encourage students to think that with effort they are able to control their behaviour and by doing so increase their own self-efficacy. Students are encouraged to attribute behavioural changes to their efforts and not as due to factors beyond their control.

Anger management (E.L. Feindler and R.B. Ecton)

Anger and aggression are seen as learned behaviours and as maintained through consequences and reinforcement. Anger involves both physiological and cognitive processes. The cognitive approach emphasises the influence of cognitive appraisal in experiencing and acting on anger. Aggressive children have a tendency to identify threats or provocative acts even when they do not exist. They are also hypervigilant in looking out for verbal and physical threats and will tend to identify ambiguous situations as threatening.

Cognitive approaches aim at self-control of anger and aggression through cognitive-mediation and arousal reduction techniques. Assessment is through self-monitoring procedures (e.g. anger log or diary) and through observation (e.g. using the ABC). Anger-management procedures are as follows:

- The student is asked to identify associated thoughts, feelings and actions. This is undertaken in order for the student to record and rate them in terms of a functional or ABC analysis.

- The aims of anger management should be stated and explained, i.e. to increase self-control over anger and to avoid anger-provoking situations.

- The student should be trained in self-instruction techniques, e.g. using positive verbal self-commands or coping statements in preparation for anger arousal and for when anger arousal is actually experienced. Role-play is useful in providing a safe space for students to practise self-instructional techniques.

- Thinking-ahead techniques are also useful. The student is asked to think of cues that are likely to elicit both anger and aggression along with future negative consequences of anger and aggression.

- Students should be trained in assertiveness, that is to affirm their legitimate rights in an assertive instead of aggressive manner.

- Students should also be trained in relaxation techniques in order to reduce anger arousal.

- The student should also be trained in self-assessment, self-reinforcement and self-evaluation. Students are asked to keep an anger log or diary and to assess and provide feedback on their responses.

Students may experience failure in anger management for the following reasons: lack of commitment, lack of necessary social skills, cognitive deficits, peer group culture, high levels of anxiety and technique problems.

Cognitive constructivism and reconstruction (G. Kelly)

Kelly's personal construct theory (1955) is based on the idea that people construct their own realities or views of the world. These are seen as personal constructions or constructs. External events are perceptually the same for everybody but the personal constructs applied to the same situation may be different depending on a particular individual's personal construct system. Personal meanings are attached to the same events resulting in different thoughts and behaviours, in effect different experiences. People are able to and do change their personal constructs for alternative constructions. New experiences lead people to change their constructs. People formulate self-constructs that they apply to themselves; these self-constructs are also amenable to change. In essence people are seen as hypotheses testers about themselves, others and the world.

Problem behaviours arise because people persist with personal constructs that are no longer valid or applicable. Personal constructs may be too few or too broad and therefore do not take into consideration subtle differences. For example, a teacher with excessively permeable constructs (very broad constructs) will not admit that students might be different.

Changing behaviour is construed in terms of developing improved personal construct systems. Treatment is defined in terms of reconstructing a personal construct system, for example by replacing constructs and including new ones.

Teachers should aim to replace their students' invalid key constructs with valid ones that allow alternatives. A student may construe other students as always having hostile intentions towards him. The aim of the teacher would be to replace the student's negative construct of hostility with one that was positive by encouraging the student to identify friendly encounters that had occurred in the past.

Cognitive evaluation

Cognitive evaluation will focus on changes in cognitive processes that have occurred during the intervention, some form of cognitive restructuring. This means identifying positive changes in students' beliefs, attitudes, expectations, attributions, personal constructs and perceived self-efficacy. Positive changes in cognitive processes will hopefully be associated with appropriate changes in behaviour. Behavioural evaluation will help to establish that changes in behaviour have also occurred.

Positive changes in students' cognitive processes occur where students believe that within themselves they have the power to change their behaviours or where students no longer blame others for their problems.

A pre-intervention baseline should be established in terms of students' beliefs, attitudes, expectations, attributions, perceived self-efficacy and personal constructs. This will enable comparisons to be made at a later date after the intervention has been terminated. There may have been positive changes, no changes or negative changes in students' cognitive processes.

| Date ⬭ Day ⬭ |
| Period ⬭ Lesson ⬭ |

Did you arrive on time?

| *Yes* | *Nearly* | *No* |

Did anybody bother you?	Did you keep your temper?
A bit/A lot	*Yes/No*
A bit/A lot	*Yes/No*
A bit/A lot	*Yes/No*
A bit/A lot	*Yes/No*
A bit/A lot	*Yes/No*

Could you do the work?

| *Not much* | *Some* | *Most* |

What did you do well?

Figure 3.7 Cognitive evaluation sheet

The social learning perspective

Social learning model

This perspective developed by Bandura (1977) and Mischel (1973) sees learning as not simply being the result of classical and operant conditioning but as being influenced by observational learning. Observational learning takes place when people learn from observing the actions of others and the consequences of those actions. People also learn to inhibit or disinhibit their actions through observing other people. Reinforcement according to this model depends on cognitive processes, namely those of anticipation and expectation. People anticipate and expect reinforcement. Therefore reinforcement is seen as dependent on cognition. Bandura introduced the concept of vicarious reinforcement, where people think about and anticipate the outcomes of observed behaviours prior to imitating those behaviours. Learning by observing does not require reinforcement as, having learned the behaviour, people decide whether to perform the behaviour or not. Bandura moved away from reinforcement contingencies to the idea that people can choose reinforcement.

Bandura and Mischel see behaviour, cognition and the environment as interconnected and as influencing each other. This three-factor interaction is called *reciprocal determinism*. This means that people's behaviours influence their environment. Their environment influences their behaviours. Their cognitions influence and are influenced by their behaviours and their environment. Therefore behaviour is seen as being the result of a plurality of causes and interactions.

The concept of self-efficacy

The key concept is perceived self-efficacy or feelings of personal competence or mastery. Self-efficacy is based on the following factors:

- *enactive attainments* are what people actually achieve or fail to achieve, these successes and failures having a powerful influence on expectations;

- *vicarious observation* of others' successes and failures affects people's expectations of their own likely successes or failures in similar situations;

- *persuasion* is not very effective in increasing self-efficacy, as telling people they can or cannot perform a given behaviour is remote from the actual situation they will experience;

- *physiological state* or the level of arousal people experience can affect their performance; overwhelming anxiety can inhibit performances of required behaviours whereas low levels of anxiety can induce people to make greater efforts to perform behaviours;

- *integration of efficacy information* is when people integrate information based on enactive attainments, vicarious observation, persuasion and physiological state. Different people will give different weights to these factors and as a result arrive at different ideas as to their self-efficacy.

There are two kinds of expectations, efficacy and outcome. *Efficacy expectations* are based on people's estimations as to whether they have the skills or resources to perform required behaviours. *Outcome expectations* are estimations as to whether outcomes will occur if personal resources and skills are applied to the problem.

Bandura regards self-efficacy as playing a major part in influencing people's behaviours and their levels of psychological functioning. High self-efficacy is seen as leading to an increase in positive behaviours and educational achievement. Parents, peers and teachers are seen as influencing student behaviour through producing high or low levels of self-efficacy. For example, teachers who communicate to their students that they are of low ability or are always badly behaved may well help induce low levels of self-efficacy in their students. As a result students may give up trying altogether.

Student behaviour is seen as influenced by the following factors.

1. The *goals* or plans they have – in terms of choosing particular priorities and actions.

2. Their *self-concept* – this refers to particular cognitive processes, e.g. self-control, self-reinforcement and self-evaluation.

3. Their *self-efficacy perceptions*, i.e. perceived capability of coping with particular problems in specific contexts; these perceptions influence students' thoughts, feelings, motivation and actions.

4. *Observational learning* – the form of learning where students learn by observing others' behaviours; the person observed is termed a model and this form of learning depends on a number of conditions:

   - *attention* – that is on the models students choose to attend to and the accuracy of their perceptions of the models' behaviour;
   - *retention* – that is on how much students remember for the purposes of practising or rehearsing the modelled behaviours;
   - *motor reproduction* – students need to possess the relevant learning skills in order to reproduce the models' behaviour;
   - *motivation* – the students' motivation to reproduce the models' behaviour.

   This form of learning is seen as explaining the origins of new behaviours.

5. *Vicarious learning* – this form of learning occurs when students acquire thoughts and feelings after observing and identifying with particular models.

6. *Self-regulation* occurs when student behaviour is regulated or influenced by expectancy or anticipation regarding future events. *Outcome expectations* are where students estimate that their behaviours will result in certain outcomes or consequences. *Efficacy expectations* are where students believe they can successfully perform certain behaviours.

Self-regulatory processes include self-observation, self-recording, self-judgement and self-reaction. Students are encouraged to observe their performances, record those performances and evaluate them in relation to previous performances.

7. Self-reinforcement occurs when students' behaviours are self-reinforced or self-rewarded according to the goals they set themselves.

Evaluation of the social learning perspective

This perspective highlights the role of expectancies and self-efficacy in influencing behaviour and behavioural change. Modelling or observational learning is seen as another type of learning alongside that of reinforcement. It is also seen as an explanation for the origins of new behaviour, particularly with reference to aggression, parental influence and the influence of the mass media on children. This perspective has been critical of behaviourist, psychoanalytic and trait theories of behaviour. Reinforcement is not seen as necessary as people can learn through observing others. Behaviour is activated by expectancies and then maintained or terminated by its consequences. Emotional and behavioural problems are seen as being caused by low levels of perceived self-efficacy. The main aim of interventions is to increase self-efficacy. Social learning theory has been criticised for giving little significance to development, motivation and conflict.

Social learning assessment

Social learning assessment focuses on describing students' levels of perceived self-efficacy and expectancies. This involves looking at students' statements about their perceived self-efficacy and associated behaviours. Statements of self-efficacy are seen as predicting levels of performance. Efficacy expectations are obtained before and after intervention. Comparisons are made in order to find out if there are increases or decreases in students' self-efficacy.

Social learning formulation

Students' problem behaviours are seen as being the result of:

- low levels of self-efficacy or feelings of inefficacy;
- exposure to models displaying negative behaviour;
- negative expectancies;
- negative self-conceptions;
- negative self-evaluations.

Anxiety is seen as being caused by perceived inefficacy, expectations of not being able to cope with threatening situations or people. The more self-efficacy can be increased the greater the reduction in anxiety.

Social learning interventions

The aims of social learning intervention are to increase both cognitive and behavioural competencies. The two main interventions are modelling and changing perceived self-efficacy.

Modelling

Modelling has the following characteristics:

- it is structured in steps or stages;

- it incorporates feedback;

- it has to be clear and easily understood;

- students rehearse until satisfactory levels of competence are reached.

Modelling can serve various functions, e.g. inhibiting or disinhibiting performance and in facilitating appropriate or inappropriate responses. Through observing appropriate models students do learn to acquire skills and strategies. Models also convey a message of success if students follow a demonstrated sequence of actions. Students can learn through cognitive modelling or direct instruction. Cognitive modelling requires teachers to verbalise their problem-solving procedures.

Teachers demonstrate the desired behaviours to students and students imitate the behaviours until they reach a satisfactory level of competence. Teachers should also comment on the demonstration while delivering it. In addition teachers may need to reinforce the students' efforts. Students should be encouraged to use positive self-statements in order to increase motivation. Peer modelling can also be effective when students observe other students mastering problems.

To be effective the model should possess the following characteristics, that is be realistic, convey trust, be convincing and have sufficient status in the eyes of students.

Changing perceived self-efficacy

Students may experience low levels of self-efficacy. This means they feel unable to perform desired behaviours, thinking they do not have the necessary resources or skills. The aim of this intervention would be to increase students' self-efficacy, i.e. feeling that they have or can acquire the skills and resources necessary to achieve the desired targets. Changing self-efficacy could be achieved through modelling, self-instructional statements, self-reinforcement and attribution retraining.

Social learning evaluation

Evaluation from this perspective primarily involves identifying and recording changes in perceived self-efficacy following interventions, i.e. from lower to higher levels of efficacy, sufficient to bring about significant behavioural change. The effectiveness of observational learning and modelling can also be evaluated. Changes in self-efficacy should be significant enough for students to feel that they have achieved a sense of personal control and competence. As a result they should now be able to acquire and utilise coping skills with respect to problem behaviour.

5 | The psychodynamic perspective

Introduction

The *psychodynamic perspective* of behaviour locates the origin of the maladaptive behaviour in the *unconscious functioning of the psyche*. Due to considerations of volume, this chapter is restricted to outlining a limited number of concepts derived from the *psychoanalytical approach*. Our intention is to give the reader an introduction to the complex area of psychoanalytical theory as it relates to emotional and behavioural difficulties in the learning situation. Those readers interested in further study will find the bibliography useful.

We have chosen to concentrate on certain aspects of psychoanalytical theory which have a more immediate relevance to the learning situation in what they have to offer us as practising teachers. We have grouped these under the heading of 'Aspects of psychoanalytical approaches and their implications for the learning situation' (see pp. 47–56)

This chapter *does not provide a guide to assessment and intervention* in the same way that the other chapters in this volume do. The previous chapters are useful in assisting the classroom practitioner and the institution in developing and evaluating interventions without considerable input from the specialist. Here, in contrast, we hope to offer a succinct guide to which aspects of psychoanalytical theory have relevance to day-to-day practice in the classroom and the larger institution of the school and which may assist those responsible for the management of schools, and teachers to reflect on preventative approaches. *Intervention in the fullest sense may ultimately remain the domain of the trained specialist.* We do, however, make a reference to the basis upon which assessment and intervention may be framed (see Table 5.1). It is hoped that the reader will gain a perspective from which to reflect on what may be occurring in the learning situation. This may enable the practitioner, through increased understanding, to manage better the stress which working with these pupils can create.

Introduction to the theory of the psychodynamic perspective

When engaged in the teaching of pupils whose behavioural difficulties originate in large part from maladaptive responses to the resolution of unconscious conflict (*psychodynamic perspective*), as opposed to maladaptive learning (*behavioural perspective*), maladaptive thinking (*cognitive/behavioural perspective*) or negative interactions (*ecosystemic perspective*), the class teacher may feel, quite appropriately,

44

Table 5.1 Application of the psychodynamic perspective to the learning situation

Perspective schema	*Psychodynamic*	*Application to learning situation*
Theoretical basis	Unconscious processes seeking resolution of psychic conflict, e.g. ego defences. Unconscious phantasy influences behaviour	Aspects of the learning situation trigger unconscious processes; pupil still enmeshed in emotional conflict generated by earlier experiences
Model of the person	Behaviour is determined by unconscious processes	Behaviour has a meaning of which the pupil is not consciously aware but which directs/influences perceptions of self, others and the learning task
Assessment basis	Ego defences; unconscious phantasy; internal working model(s)	Defences; aspects of the interpersonal relationship between pupil and teacher, pupil and peers, pupil and school; characteristics of engagement with the learning task
Assessment procedure	Projective techniques, transference-relationship; defences/unconscious phantasies inferred	Observation schedules; learning profiles; quality of engagement in the learning task; interviews; projective techniques; pupil's use of metaphor; transference-relationship with teacher and peers
Formulation basis	Unresolved unconscious conflicts/phantasies/inappropriate internal working models manifest in emotional and behavioural difficulties	Learning difficulties arise from unresolved emotional difficulties caused by unconscious conflicts or pre-occupations
Formulation	Problem behaviour caused by unresolved unconscious conflicts/phantasies/internal working model arousing unconscious anxiety and ego defences	Aspects of the learning situation trigger anxiety. Maladaptive response has an unconscious component
Intervention basis	Facilitating insight; strengthening the ego	Identifying and modifying where inappropriate aspects of the learning situation which arouse pupil's anxiety. Increasing pupil's confidence ability to manage aspects of the learning situation. Increase self-esteem
Intervention strategies	Interpretation of resistances and defences or unconscious phantasy in and through the transference-relationship	Working at one remove through use of metaphor; voicing pupil's feelings; play therapy, art, music and educational therapy; reducing threatening aspects of the learning situations; promoting self-esteem
Evaluation basis	Insight into unconscious conflict; ego-strength	Modification of maladaptive aspects of pupil's engagement in the learning situation as a result of emotional pre-occupations
Evaluation	Increased insight and ego-strength	Improved management of response to anxiety in the learning situation; more appropriate interaction with teacher and peers. More attention available to engage in learning task

that the training they have received as teachers does not fully equip them to deal with the challenges which this particular type of pupil behaviour can present. Indeed, as previously stated, these pupils often need specialised interventions in order to facilitate meaningful behavioural change in the learning situation.

In *psychoanalytical theory* the origin of the emotional and behavioural difficulty is located in the earliest history of the child's development. The experiences encountered and unconscious phenomena (e.g. ego defences, unconscious phantasy – see below) which children have developed during this period, and which inform their perceptions of outer reality, are filtered through their inner world of emotions. These have remained, in part, unchanged or have failed to adapt to real change in the outer world. The outer reality continues to be interpreted and processed as though it were in fact still part of the infantile/child's world. Events in the objective world of the older child trigger reactions which seem in many cases to belong to the behavioural repertoire of the infant or young child. From this perspective, the manifest behaviour is not perceived as a direct response to what is occurring objectively, but as related unconsciously to much earlier experience.

The psychodynamic approach is concerned with applying principles derived from psychoanalytical theory in an attempt to understand the meaning which pupils invest in their understanding of the world. It is this which underlies aspects of their maladaptive behaviour. This meaning is not always accessible through the assessment techniques which apply in the other perspectives outlined elsewhere in this volume. Psychoanalytical theory is extremely complex and there are many differences of opinion and debate around the functions and roles of the processes of the psyche. In what follows, we have aimed at giving the non-specialist an overview of those parts of the theory which have perhaps more relevance when it comes to the learning situation.

Referral characteristics from the psychodynamic perspective

This chapter is concerned with the pupil whose behaviour may present as:

- *'incomprehensible'* or *'inconsequential'* or *'puzzling'*;

- *under-achieving* despite proven cognitive ability;

- *immature* in comparison to others of the same age;

- *phobic*;

- *anxious, withdrawn or depressed*;

- *hostile*;

- *unpredictable* in terms of actions and reactions and where no obvious pattern emerges easily.

Pupils with emotional and behavioural difficulties may also have specific learning difficulties. Unless these are assessed and specialist support given the pupil will not make progress. However, as we have said above, sometimes the failure to achieve cannot be traced to a specific learning or cognitive difficulty. It is as if such pupils are not free to use their ability because they are consciously or unconsciously preoccupied by the 'muddle' caused by the emotional problem. While these pupils remain preoccupied by unresolved inner conflict they are unable to engage in the learning situation to the best of their ability. For this reason, the emotional difficulty is as much a special educational need as that associated with a specific learning difficulty and requires that we make provision for addressing it as such.

The teachers of pupils who might be described using some of the above definitions are often left feeling:

- *de-skilled, inadequate* or *helpless* to bring about change or impart skills;

- *angry;*

- *despairing;*

- *anxious;*

- *depressed;*

- *isolated* or *'persecuted'* (as when a pupil seems to experience these difficulties with one teacher or group of teachers only and where others report no concerns).

As we will discuss later in the chapter, the way the teacher feels, or is made to feel, by this type of pupil behaviour is a significant part of the diagnostic picture. Of course, any teacher, on a 'bad' day, may feel all of the above with pupils who do not have extreme symptoms. It is the degree to which the teacher experiences these feelings, the duration of difficulty and its seeming resistance to modification or permanent change in the learning relationship which characterises the teaching of this pupil group.

Aspects of psychoanalytical approaches and their implications in the learning situation

Ego defences in the learning situation (S. Freud, A. Freud and Klein)

The theory of ego defence is most commonly associated with Sigmund Freud as the originator of the term. However, numerous other forms of ego defence were further elaborated by Freud's daughter Anna and also Melanie Klein. These are not exhaustive.

Definition of the ego

- The ego could be defined as that part of the individual's psyche which has the function of *differentiating, rationalising* or *controlling* the more primitive, un-structured or 'passionate' elements of the psyche which are experienced unconsciously as potentially overwhelming to the ego.

- The ego will also act to preserve the individual's *sense of identity* which itself is seen to have worth. It may do this when certain *unacceptable/unbearable aspects of the self* threaten to manifest

themselves. Threats to the ego's sense of worth, or to its function as a kind of psychic 'cement' to the identity of the self, are experienced as threats to the existence of the individual and arouse anxiety.

Ego defences

- The ego uses defence mechanisms (see Table 5.2) to protect its integrity and ability to continue to differentiate, rationalise or control the more primitive, unstructured or 'passionate' elements of the psyche. In other words the ego protects itself from the 'unbearable'.

- These defence mechanisms operate at an unconscious level so that the individual is not, by definition, aware of them.

- This defensive process is not seen to be maladaptive in itself. It is deemed maladaptive when the defensive response gives rise to behaviour which causes difficulties in the person's harmonious adaptation to reality.

- The degree of ego-anxiety experienced as a result of conflict will differ from one individual to another, as will mechanisms for coping with this.

- When these strategies or mechanisms are used successfully without undue disruption to the person's life, they do reduce tension. Their success reinforces their use and the person will begin to adopt positions which will have the effect of reducing ego-anxiety habitually. In other words the defences become part of what we loosely call the 'personality'.

Aspects of the learning situation which arouse ego defences

Certain aspects of the learning situation can provoke anxiety. Each act of learning requires a certain amount of risk-taking. Learning tasks can carry with them the potential for the accompanying or related risk of exposing the ego to (unbearable) anxiety, e.g. in the form of a confrontation with the individual's limitations either short- or long-term. The relationships with the teacher and peers can also provoke anxiety. Certain unconscious defences, or the degree to which they are used to defend against this anxiety, can hinder progress in the learning situation. The examples below indicate some aspects of the learning situation which may result in maladaptive responses arising from the unconscious defence used to cope with the anxiety.

Potential triggers of ego-defences

IN THE LEARNING TASK
- a task in which pupils feels unconfident and where their sense of self-worth might be challenged through being seen to make mistakes;

- persevering with a difficult task which involves the management of frustration and lack of immediate gratification;

- feeling impotent or belittled in the face of not knowing;

- tasks or topics which might bring pupils into unconscious contact with aspects of their inner and outer life which create anxiety.

Table 5.2 Examples of common ego defences used in the learning situation

Defence	Definition	Example in the learning situation
Regression	Process whereby the individual avoids or seeks to avoid anxiety by partial or total return to an earlier stage of development	A pupil will revert to an immature mode of behaviour, e.g. crying or rolling around on the floor in order to avoid tackling a task which he/she feels they will not be able to accomplish
Denial	Denying or forgetting painful feelings and events	Pupils who might be experiencing difficulty with a task will defend themselves from feelings of belittlement by denying the difficulty and avoiding the task. For example: 'This is too easy for me. This is baby stuff.'
Splitting	When people are denying unacceptable parts of themselves, they may go on to use the defence of splitting this unacceptable part off and projecting it on to someone else. Splitting may also be used to describe the process whereby two or more significant others are endowed with opposing characteristics	Pupils might accuse the teacher or a classmate of being e.g. hostile towards them when they are in fact feeling anxious about their own unconscious hostility towards them. The pupil's hostility is said to be split off. The pupil might behave towards one teacher(s) as if they are wonderful and towards another (others) as if they are awful
Projection	When people experience impulses or wishes or aspects of themselves which are unacceptable, they might situate these in another (see denial)	Victims of bullying might be projecting their own aggressive impulses on to the bully
Idealisation	Idealisation might result in part from a mixture of denial, splitting and projection. The need for a perfect other results in the denial of less wonderful parts of the person. Idealisation is a defence against recognising faults in the other towards which one might experience envious or hostile or some other unacceptable feeling. By idealising the other one is freed from the guilt of these negative feelings but the result is a loss of self-esteem through comparison with the other	Pupils may not reach their full potential in the learning situation where they feel unconscious envy of another pupil's success. This is defended against by idealising that pupil and belittling themselves in comparison. The other is better or even perfect and cannot be competed with
Rationalisation	A process of giving an explanation for an action after the event in order to conceal its true motivation to oneself and others	Pupils who explain a failure to bring in homework because they had forgotten to take the right material home in the first place and thereby rationalise their own lack of responsibility or anxiety about being able to fulfil the task
Reaction-formation	This is a defence where an unacceptable impulse is controlled by exaggerating its opposite	A pupil who is extremely tidy might be concealing an inner feling of messiness and 'unpresentability'

Note: The above list is not exhaustive; it can be seen that one defence tends to lead to another.

IN THE RELATIONSHIP WITH THE TEACHER
- having a new or temporary teacher where the boundaries and expectations are still unclear;

- experiencing aspects of the teacher's role as reminiscent of aspects of other significant person's roles in the pupil's life (see transference and attachment below);

- being unsure about whether the teacher values the pupil as a person (see internal working models below);

- experiencing the teacher as comparatively more powerful or knowing and envying what knowledge, ability and skill they possess (see unconscious phantasies below).

IN RELATIONSHIPS WITH PEERS
- not being able to master a new concept as quickly or as well as one's peers;

- being able to master a task far better than one's peers and therefore giving rise to their envy;

- experiencing feelings of rivalry for the attention of the teacher or other significant person.

All of us use ego defences. Most of the time these defences cause little or no disruption to the learning process. However, the anxiety in some children before a new task or a return to one which has caused past anxiety can be extreme and give rise to a more intense and resistant ego-defence mechanism over which simple encouragement and support will have little or no effect.

Transference as a defence in the learning situation (S. Freud, A. Freud, Klein)

Definition of transference

Transference is the psychoanalytical term used to describe the phenomenon whereby the client in analysis unconsciously endows the analyst with characteristics belonging to significant persons from the client's past. Transference occurs in relationships with other important figures in the person's life. A pupil may well bring transference into the relationship with the teacher.

Transference may be positive (where the person is endowed with attributes of a significant past figure which the individual has experienced as positive), or negative (where the person is endowed with attributes which the individual has experienced as negative).

Transference as a defence in the learning situation

- A common behaviour with pupils who have emotional or behavioural difficulties is seen in what teachers often call 'testing-out'. This might be seen to originate in the pupil's past experience of relationships with significant people. For example, pupils who have experienced rejection may not at first respond to a teacher's attempts to form a positive relationship with them. Instead these pupils may go through a period of testing out where they stand with the teacher. Such pupils may in effect be trying to bring about positive responses from the teacher and their testing-out behaviour needs to be seen in this light. It is as if the pupil is wondering if this teacher is 'just like all the other adults'. If pupils have been emotionally hurt by adults in the past they need to 'test out' whether this adult will repeat that interaction.

An example of how an ego defence might hinder learning

John is a 10-year-old in NC Year 6. He has an average IQ and has no specific learning difficulty. However he is at the beginning stages of reading and writing and uses diversionary tactics of disruption to avoid the anxiety he experiences when he is confronted with a task which he feels unable to manage. In fact, John has recourse to a number of ego defences but here we shall concentrate on his use of regression.

At the start of the NC Year 6, after the summer holidays, John refused to return to school and ended up being literally dragged in, kicking and screaming, by his mother. When she felt able to leave, he collapsed in the corridor outside his classroom and began to wail loudly 'I want my mummy.' He was behaving very much as some children do when they are taken to nursery school and left there for the first time. It took weeks to settle John back into class, during which time he was able to avoid 'work' almost entirely, having a special programme set up for him where he was able to work at the level of a Reception child for the most part. In some ways then John achieved relief from the anxiety of failure by regressing to this earlier stage of ego development. However, this was achieved at the price of simultaneously re-activating the much earlier anxieties of this stage connected to separation from his mother (see the section on attachment). In connection with this it is perhaps relevant that from the age of three, John's parents' relationship began to break down ending in divorce with father leaving the family home when John was in Reception. As he never progressed much beyond this stage in terms of academic achievement, it would appear that his emotional and intellectual development became 'stuck' at this point.

- Transference, insofar as it projects unconscious feelings or intentions on to the other, can also be used as an ego defence. This may result in a projection on to the teacher of feelings which the pupil might be finding unbearable. Earlier in the chapter we indicated that the way a teacher may be made to feel by certain pupils can provide information about what might be happening in emotional terms for the pupil. For example, a pupil who repeatedly makes a teacher feel deskilled, hopeless, furious or confused etc. may be using the transference to 'put into' the teacher feelings which the pupil experiences in the learning situation which arouse anxiety and are alleviated by making the teacher feel them in his place. This could be seen in some ways as an unconscious attempt on the part of the pupil to communicate these unbearable feelings to the teacher. It is as if the pupil has an unconscious belief that if the teacher 'knows' how the pupil is feeling then she will be in a better position to understand the true nature of his emotional needs and thus be better placed to cater for them.

The value of standing back

There is an intensity of feeling and a kind of 'predictability' about the interactions between the pupil and the teacher in the transference that is a good indicator that this is what is at work. It may be very hard for the teacher to resist falling into the trap of behaving towards the pupil in a certain way; the way he is unconsciously manipulating her to behave. Take for example the phenomenon of losing one's temper with a certain pupil continually and despite one's better professional judgement. Somehow we find ourselves doing it again and again even when we suspect that this is the aim (conscious or not) of the pupil (who will then sit back and enjoy it). This is a fairly banal but common example of how transference might be at work. It may indicate that the pupil has feelings of unbearable frustration and danger under the cover of bored or insolent indifference and he is projecting these feelings onto the teacher literally making her feel them. The value of looking at the interaction in this way is that it may enable the teacher to stand back.

Instead of being 'fooled' by the pupil's overt behaviour the teacher may be able to look at the elements in the learning situation which may be arousing his frustration and anger. Is the pupil covering up real difficulties with learning? Does the pupil feel that his self-esteem is at risk? Does he feel that his needs are not being met? By asking questions about what might lie behind the behaviour we may be able to shift the dynamics of the interaction. Discussing with other colleagues in a supportive climate how a particular pupil makes the teacher feel can help to throw some light on what is occurring. It may be that the pupil has the same effect on the colleague or the colleague has had similar feelings about other pupils.

Unconscious phantasy and the learning situation (Klein)

Definition of unconscious phantasy

- According to psychoanalytical thinking, infants, from the beginning of life, develop unconscious phantasies about all that they experience. (This does not refer to 'fantasies' of the day-dreaming type or conscious imaginings – hence the use of the different spelling.)

- Since the infant experiences most vividly through their bodily sensations and functions, these phantasies are, in the first instance, constructed from the biological processes of, for example, feeding, digestion and defecation. The infant develops certain phantasies around the experience of the mother, or rather her body. He does not, to begin with, experience her as a whole person but rather as parts of a body: the breast (or bottle which represents the breast), the face, etc.

- Certain unconscious phantasies may arouse anxiety which the ego seeks to master by developing defences (see above).

- As the infant grows and his mental processes develop, these unconscious phantasies do not cease to be active. Psychoanalytical theory maintains that these unconscious phantasies accompany conscious thought and indeed affect it throughout life.

An example of unconscious phantasy

As we have stated above, unconscious phantasy is attached to all aspects of the infant's experience. Here, we look at some aspects of the phantasies around the infant's experience of feeding in particular. In the unconscious phantasy of the infant, the breast (or bottle) is experienced as the source of all that is good and nourishing, and, when this experience of feeding is good, it is associated in phantasy with life-giving properties.

The breast is further experienced in unconscious phantasy as possessing something desirable and the mother who 'owns' the breast is felt to enjoy all the goodness which the breast bestows. Through the operation of this phantasy, the infant may come to envy the breast which the mother seems to be able to have 'all to herself'. The infant in relation to this may unconsciously experience a sense of lack of control and hostility towards the breast/mother and consequent anxiety and development of ego defences.

Examples of unconscious phantasy around feeding in the learning situation

We have chosen to concentrate here on the unconscious phantasies associated with the feeding experience. There are many others but space compels us to select.

When the child is in the learning situation the unconscious phantasies which accompanied the act of feeding, digesting, defecating etc. may come to be associated with, and affect, the act of taking in knowledge from the teacher.

In order to learn, the pupil has at some point to experience his lack of knowledge, his need for it, or his 'hunger' for it. The pupil may be unable to bear this feeling of 'not knowing' and of being dependent on the teacher. The teacher possesses the desired knowledge and enjoys the benefits while the pupil is diminished by comparison.

Certain pupils may have developed negative unconscious phantasies around the early experience of feeding. Through association, the dependency on the teacher for the 'nourishment' of knowledge may, for example, arouse feelings of intense envy which originate in the unconscious phantasy.

The pupil may defend against the envious, angry feelings by 'rubbishing' overtly what the teacher has to offer or deprive the envied teacher the satisfaction of seeing the good which her knowledge or skill can bring to the pupil. Rather than experience her as a source of nourishment and therefore an object of envy, he protects himself from the feelings of belittlement or 'not having' or 'not knowing' by perceiving what she has to offer as worthless.

A pupil who experiences the teacher in this way may characteristically have the unconscious phantasy of being able to 'feed' himself and therefore not need to take in any learning from the teacher. Such a child may leave the teacher feeling deskilled, with nothing to offer. When a teacher systematically feels this kind of disparagement despite having real skills, there is a very good chance that envy is at work here. Indeed, the pupil is somehow communicating to the teacher by making her feel the unbearable feelings which he experiences in the learning situation. The teacher feels she has nothing to offer, that her skills are just not 'up to the mark', that she does not know what to do here. Ironically, the better the teacher, the more they may actually feel this. The pupil would not experience the impulse to spoil had he not perceived that there was something 'good' there to envy in the first place.

Other pupils while not openly 'rubbishing' what the teacher has to offer may nevertheless fail to make progress. Envy may also be at work here. The pupil cannot take the risk of giving the teacher the pleasure of seeing him make use of what she has to offer. If she cannot enjoy what she has to offer, the pupil need not feel envious of her ability to 'feed' him knowledge.

The pupil's own experience of envy can be so intense and anxiety-provoking due to the unconscious association with infantile experience, that he may defend against the envy he may himself provoke in others if he is successful. Fear of others' envy can also hinder the pupil's learning progress and contribute to chronic under-achievement.

In extreme cases where a negative unconscious phantasy influences the perceptions of the pupil in the learning situation, the child may not be able to take in anything good from the learning experience. This pupil might need intensive therapeutic help.

Effect of emotional deprivation and loss in the learning situation (Bowlby)

It has been objected by some psychoanalytical theorists (Bowlby *et al.*) that the psychoanalytical perspective on child development places the emphasis almost exclusively on the content of the phantasy life of the child while denying the extent and influence of real life events on the development and the origin of maladaptive responses. However, the frame of reference when looking at the effects of deprivation of primary care or loss on the cognitive and emotional development of the child remains that of psychoanalysis (including the use of ego defences).

Attachment theory and emotional deprivation and loss

- Clinical observations of the universal characteristics of the behaviour of infants when they became separated from their mother (or permanent primary care-giver) provided the basis for *attachment theory*.

- There is a critical time in very early infancy when babies formed a bond with their primary care-giver (parent or permanent parent substitute). This bond is termed *'attachment'*.

- Attachment is observable when the baby behaves in a way which is designed to bring the primary care-giver or *attachment figure* to them (searching for eye-contact, crying etc.).When babies are older (around 8–10 months), this attachment manifests itself in behaviour which tends to direct the baby towards the care-giver (reaching out, running towards, clinging etc.). These behaviours are called *attachment behaviours*.

- When babies are separated from their attachment figure they manifest behaviour which is called *separation anxiety*. This anxiety is experienced when attachment behaviour is activated (e.g. the attachment figure leaves the baby behind with a stranger or alone, or baby experiences fear and mother is not actually present etc.) but cannot be shut off or terminated (e.g. when the attachment figure is not immediately available).

The aim of attachment behaviour is to seek the presence of the attachment figure and the *assuaging of the anxiety* which the separation aroused.

Secure attachment

- When the attachment figure is able to respond appropriately to the infant's attachment behaviour, the infant's anxiety is relieved or assuaged. *Responding appropriately* might include actual holding or cuddling of the infant when they need to be reassured or comforted and doing this in a consistent way which arises from the *real needs of the child*.

- The infant comes to learn that he has a *reliable attachment figure* who is available for him and whose actions have a certain amount of predictability. The infant builds a picture of meaningful behaviour with trusted adults. Secure attachment gives the child what is called a *'secure base'*.

- If the infant has a secure base he is freed to go on to develop behaviours such as exploration of the environment. This particular behaviour is essential if the *learning potential* of the child is to have a chance of fulfilment.

- Through his interactions with the attachment figure, the infant develops what is termed an *'internal working model'*.

- In the case of secure attachment this internal working model equips the child with a picture of himself as a worthwhile individual. This 'worthwhileness' has been demonstrated by the *continual and affirming interaction* between himself and the attachment figure.

Insecure attachment or loss of an attachment figure

- An infant might come to develop an insecure or anxious attachment when the attachment figure is *not emotionally available* to him significantly or repeatedly. (Extreme examples of this might be when the attachment figure is chronically depressed, ill or intensely preoccupied by inner or outer experiences).

- When the attachment figure is unable, for whatever reason, to respond appropriately to the infant's attachment behaviour, the child develops an internal working model of *self-doubt and depreciation*.

- He is unable to build up an experience of *consistent or meaningful relationships*. He may not feel safe enough to express negative feelings towards the attachment figure, e.g. anger, frustration.

- These feelings may through the process of *defence mechanisms* (see above) be displaced on to significant others (e.g. teachers).

- Responding appropriately does not only mean giving the infant reassurance when he needs it. It can be just as inappropriate to give the infant so much reassurance that he never has the opportunity to learn to deal gradually with the inevitable frustrations of real life. He may be *over-protected*.

- In the case of insecure attachment, there is no secure base from which to explore the world around them and he is *less likely to achieve his full potential* in the learning situation.

When a child suffers a *permanent loss* of an attachment figure through death or family break-up, their ability to manage and achieve the reorganisation of the personality which is necessary to adapt to the situation will be easier in the case of a child who has had the experience of secure attachment rather than insecure attachment.

Implications of attachment theory in the learning situation

- Securely attached children are better able to take the risk of exploring new 'territory'. This is a necessary condition for the acquisition of new knowledge and skills.

- Children with a positive experience of attachment will more readily make positive new attachments, e.g. to their teacher(s).

- Expectations of interaction with adults are positive and affirming of their own worth. They are more likely to be able to form stable and caring relationships with adults and to elicit positive and caring responses from them. They will be able to seek help when they are experiencing difficulty in the academic or social context in the classroom as their early experience of vulnerability is one of sensitive adult response to their need. They will possess a greater capacity for tolerating the inevitable frustrations of the process of learning. They will not feel threatened at having to share the attention of these adults with peers. Not being preoccupied with unresolved attachment problems, they are free to concentrate on the learning task and have a better chance of reaching their full potential.

- The converse is true to a greater or lesser degree in children who have formed insecure attachments.

- Intervention in the case of children whose emotional difficulties may stem from insecure attachment are based on attempts to modify the *internal working model* which the child carries with him. The more negative messages the child carries about himself, the more that child needs positive messages from significant others (class teachers among them) to alter these perceptions. Interventions based on the aim of raising the pupil's *self-esteem* and providing *clear boundaries* which offer an experience of *consistent interaction* are appropriate in this context.

Examples of insecure attachment in the learning situation

- *School phobia* has been linked to the existence of insecure attachment. Concerns for the well-being of the attachment figure in their absence or the lack of a secure emotional base may make the child anxious when he has to leave the attachment figure. This child may be incapable of making positive new attachments to his teacher. (The example of John also illustrates insecure attachment. His behaviour when mother left him in school on the first day back could be seen as a manifestation of separation anxiety.)

- There are aspects of the learning situation which can be experienced in an unconsciously symbolic way as linked to *the fear of abandonment* and activating similar responses. For example, when children do form attachments to the teacher, the imminent 'loss' of that teacher as at transition times from class to class or school to school or even during breaks in the school year can raise anxiety in children whose original attachment figure is/was unable to provide a secure attachment or base.

- *Beginnings and endings* can be particularly charged with difficulty for pupils with emotional and behavioural difficulties. On a large scale, beginning a new academic year or ending an old one can raise anxiety around e.g. 'not knowing' or of being 'abandoned'. How these events are approached can make a significant difference to these pupils.

- If a child is carrying an internal working model of self-doubt and depreciation, he may unconsciously set out to prove that this is the 'right' model each time he meets with new people, for example teachers. This child may provoke negative reactions in the teacher and thus reinforce these feelings of self-doubt and worthlessness.

Preventative measures in schools

Given that our pupils come to us with inner working models and habitual defensive responses to the experiences they have built up already, they may be more or less well-equipped to deal with the many demands of the learning situation and the anxieties which these may arouse at an unconscious level, some of which we have explored in the chapter.

Some pupils will have failed to resolve unconscious conflict effectively and are still enmeshed in the emotional difficulties this has caused and continues to cause. The attention which should be available for learning is therefore tied up with these preoccupations. These pupils have special educational needs which, until they are addressed, will continue to interfere with their access to and progress through the learning situation which reflects their true ability. When these needs are addressed successfully, the emotional energy or attention hitherto taken up by the unconscious emotional conflict or anxiety is released and the pupil is enabled to direct this towards making progress in the learning situation. By providing a secure environment which is responsive to the emotional needs of these pupils, schools can help.

Success in the learning situation, though sometimes very hard won for these pupils and their teachers, can strengthen the pupil's capacity to overcome difficulties and the resulting increase in self-worth and ability to adapt can have far-reaching effects. Our tendency as teachers is to become overwhelmed by the emotional trauma and deprivation which we know some of our pupils experience on a day-to-day basis outside school. However, each new encounter with a significant other (e.g. a teacher) is an opportunity to re-work the inner model or modify the defence. Through an awareness of how the learning task might be experienced as anxiety-provoking for all pupils, not just those with emotional and behavioural difficulties, schools can take measures to provide a secure and emotionally (and physically) unthreatening environment. This can go some way towards enabling the ego to perform its integrating and healing function, without, in the case of the less damaged or 'troubled' ego, recourse to specialist therapeutic intervention. Schools need to identify which agencies can provide support in meeting the special educational needs of these pupils.

Whole-school practices

Pupils with emotional and behavioural difficulties require an environment which actively seeks to reduce the incidence of potential or real anxiety and the related learning difficulties which these pupils might experience. A learning environment which offers security, consistency, clear boundaries (in terms of roles and responsibilities) and respect for individual differences can go a long way towards achieving this for a large number of pupils, including those who do not have identified emotional or behavioural difficulties. Behaving consistently, providing tasks which are set at the appropriate level for the pupil and providing clear instructions and realistic learning goals can help. Schools can also encourage an active pastoral curriculum which recognises the needs of the whole child not just the academic, in particular the need for raising and maintaining self-esteem.

Schools might also want to consider how they will support staff through training in the area of emotional and behavioural difficulties. Training in child protection would be an important consideration in this context. Active partnership with parents will also be essential if the needs of pupils with emotional and behavioural difficulties are to be met.

Metaphor in the curriculum

All pupils, not only those with emotional and behavioural difficulties, can be helped to explore their feelings, and the confusion which sometimes accompanies these, by use of appropriate stories or topics within the normal curriculum. The identification with characters, real or imaginary, can enable them to experience 'at one remove' similar conflicts and dramas in which they might find themselves. They may do this through discussion in class or creative writing or drama activities. (Although there are some books which focus specifically on feelings, most good children's books can be used in this way.) All good children's stories contain aspects of the struggle to overcome difficulties, to grow to a new understanding of the world and others and, ultimately, to accept our limitations in allowing ourselves to be who we are, 'warts and all'. As teachers, we know and return constantly to these stories with our pupils.

Maintaining boundaries

Pupils need to feel that their teachers are sincere when they communicate with them and that they are concerned and involved in their well-being. However, teachers should be alert to becoming enmeshed in their pupils' problems. A non-judgemental approach to the pupil is necessary to avoid the pupil feeling that he is worthless as a person. But this does not mean that teachers should be indulgent or collusive. The pupil who feels his points of view are listened to by the teacher is more likely to develop a positive relationship with that teacher. However, the teacher needs to be aware that empathising with the pupil may result in over-identification with him or with the teacher projecting their own problems onto the pupil. These boundaries are important as emotional stress in the teacher can result. Being in touch with the painful feelings of the pupil may trigger the teacher's own painful feelings. It is very important that staff who deal with pupils with emotional and behavioural problems should have access to non-judgemental support when, as a result of their interactions with pupils in distress, they may be left feeling emotionally drained or bruised themselves. Some special schools for pupils with EBD see supportive and regular supervision for staff as essential for their professional well-being.

Summary

The origin of present emotional and behavioural difficulties in the learning situation derives from *significant past experience* often linked to those of early infancy.

- The pupil is *not consciously aware* that the perceptions he or she brings to the present learning situation have their origin in significant past or early experience.

- The behaviour of the pupil in the present learning situation can be seen as a *metaphor for the inner reality* of the pupil, based on unconscious beliefs about the nature of the self, and of relationships, formed through past experience.

- The manifest *behaviour is meaningful* when seen as an unconscious attempt on the part of the pupil to avoid painful feelings or anxiety which are experienced as threatening to the pupil's sense of identity or self-worth.

- The defence against psychic pain or anxiety may result in a *maladaptive response* to the demands of the learning situation.

- *Interventions* are based on an assessment of the pupil's emotional and behavioural difficulties which attempt to arrive at an awareness of the possible *unconscious meaning* which the pupil might be using to interpret the present situation.

- The pupil may unconsciously bring to the relationship with the teacher(s) elements of significant past relationships which are then said to form the basis for a *transference*. The teacher may also unconsciously bring similar elements from her own past relationships to the relationship with the pupil.

- The pupil may communicate their emotional state to the teacher/carer through the unconscious process of *projection* whereby the teacher is made to feel the psychic pain which is unbearable to the pupil.

As in all manifestations of problematic behaviour, there exists a continuum and principles of prevention are relevant here. By that we mean that even where the classroom practitioner is not trained to intervene, an understanding of the dynamics of the learning situation from the point of view of the unconscious meaning these children may bring to it can help the practitioner and the institution in which he or she operates. Teachers can begin to reflect on certain practices which may unwittingly exacerbate the difficulties of these pupils and by the same token, which practices, if they were to be adopted, might contribute to an easing of the situation.

6 The humanistic perspective

It's not (so much) what you do it's the way that you do it.

Emotionally literate children have increased resilience to mental health problems.
(Mental Health Foundation, 1999).

The basis of humanistic psychology is concerned with the way people function as whole beings that have thoughts and feelings. The original concepts were formulated by psychologists such as Carl Rogers and Abraham Maslow and others, but are continually being developed and applied by many workers, some who would not identify themselves with this perspective. The field of humanistic psychology is not a clearly defined one and is characterised particularly by the values to which it holds.

Rogers' (1974) view is that to be fully human is to be in a continual state of learning and it is this idea which makes the humanistic perspective especially pertinent for schools when considering the management of behaviour. This applies to the management of staff as well as pupils.

The humanistic approach to managing behaviour tries to maximise a pupil's inherent motivation to learn by minimising factors that undermine or inhibit this process. In school, this will involve recognising that the way pupils feel about themselves and their capabilities is crucial to their success as independent learners. Maslow (1998) clarifies how needs such as physical/safety needs have to be adequately met before self-esteem even becomes an issue.

Learning is a natural process

At the core of the perspective is the view that learning is a basic drive and that the way we feel is strongly influential in the efficacy of this process. This is most importantly true about the way we feel about ourselves as a individual. This approach aims to identify factors which enhance or inhibit a pupil's ability to give their attention to the demands of the learning situation. It also reminds us that it is useful to take into account the fact that pupils are individuals with their own lives and feelings and, if we do not, we may limit the horizons of pupils as well as impede the learning process itself.

One concept developed by Rogers is 'congruency'. Where there is a lack of congruency, either within a person or between a person and their environment, there is conflict. Within the school situation this will often be revealed by inappropriate or undesirable behaviour. Maslow argues that these behaviours result from attempts on the part of the individual to meet basic needs. Maslow schematises these needs in his 'hierarchy of needs' with physiological and survival needs at the base and 'self-actualisation' (or in terms of schools, a 'fully independent learner') at the apex.

Self-esteem is concerned with the feelings that we have about ourselves and is built on feedback that we receive, particularly in our early years, from those around us. The humanistic view is that we learn best when we feel good about ourselves, or to use Rogers' term, we are able to show ourselves 'unconditional positive regard'. Goleman (1996) explores the important part feelings play in people's lives. In this book he discusses how being 'emotionally literate' is an important aspect of people's ability to learn and to apply their learning.

Minds like parachutes

Minds, like parachutes, only function when open.[1]

Humanistic psychology holds that people are 'reflexive' (John McLeod in Woolf and Dryden, 1996), i.e. able to reflect on their thoughts and their feelings in response to experience. It is this ability which allows people to have choice about their actions rather than responding automatically and rigidly to certain stimuli. Stress and threat, either in the present or as unresolved issues from the past, can reduce the individual's ability to be reflective and creative. This in turn can 'force' them into inappropriate and unsatisfactory responses to situations, which may 'work' in the short term but be counter-productive in the long term. Pupils are most likely to be reflexive when they feel safe enough and good enough about themselves to have 'open minds'.

A sense of self derives from both an individual's reflexivity and their experience of social interaction. Humanistic counselling frequently aims to reconcile the personal view of 'me' and the socially defined person that is 'me'. People learn who they are and what kind of people they are from how significant others around them react to them and treat them. The poem found in many schools, 'Children Learn What They Live' by Dorothy Law Nolte (Nolte and Harris, 1998), which includes the following lines, describes this relationship:

If children live with criticism, they learn to condemn,
If children live with hostility, they learn to fight,
If children live with approval, they learn to like themselves...

Children who develop a positive self-concept will, as they grow older, be less dependent on those around them for a sense of worth and consequently be more resilient to life's ups and downs. Initially, lack of confidence and poor self-esteem may be limited to specific areas but in the longer term, if the individual continues to experience failure and negative feedback, the 'islands' of low self-esteem can enlarge, link up and eventually pervade their entire sense of self.

Physical beings

The humanistic approach recognises that we are physical beings and when we experience the world we do so through the medium of physical bodies as much as, if not more than, our minds – *'I have a gut feeling ... You've broken my heart ... I can't*

---

[1] Notice outside the church adjacent to, what was then, Lewisham Teachers Centre

stomach this ... I've got cold feet about it ...'

Feelings are what make things seem important to us and, in this way, motivate us to action. When we feel happy we might smile and say nice things to people, when we feel lonely we might ring someone, when we feel cross we might kick the cat. Sometimes painful feelings need to be expressed directly in order to ease the discomfort or as part of the process of coming to terms with experience – when we are sad, we cry; when we are embarrassed or nervous, we laugh; when we are afraid or shocked, we tremble; when we are bored or physically tense, we yawn. This can also apply to happiness – when we are 'overjoyed' we need to tell everybody about it. (It is interesting to note that in Chinese Medicine too much joy is said to injure the heart.)

A teacher told me of a recent example of the impact of an emotional experience on learning. A pupil in her school was in Turkey, visiting his grandparents, during the recent earthquake. This child generally committed little to paper but, on returning to school, he was able to write a powerful description of his terrifying experience. He and his family were delighted when the story was reproduced in the local newspaper – which helped turn a tragedy into a positive experience.

Socialisation

Through socialisation, emotional processes are often discouraged and become over-controlled – *'big boys don't cry'* or *'nice girls don't get angry'* – leading to a lack of congruency between feelings and perception. Boys are not supposed to feel scared and so this sense of vulnerability often becomes overlaid with a layer of externally directed anger – *'the best means of defence is attack'*. It seems likely that this process may contribute to a predominance of acting-out behaviour in boys. (The end of the film *Rambo – First Blood* contains a moving scene which makes the connection between violence and the unexpressed painful emotion that underlies it.) This could also have implications for boys' abilities to listen well and to be empathic. For girls, socialisation tends to reinforce a lack of assertiveness and a socially subordinate position in society and relationships.

Expressing feelings and the need for attention

To be healthy, feelings need to be acknowledged or expressed and failure to do this adequately or appropriately can lead to 'acting-out' or withdrawn behaviour. Unreleased feelings, in the long term, can lead to both psychological conflict and physical 'dis-ease'. In order for these processes of release to occur effectively, a child has to feel safe and cared about. This is most likely to occur when parents or carers are able to give their child full, non-judgemental attention or 'unconditional positive regard'. Wipfler (1990, 1995a, 1995b) describes an approach for parents to give their full, interested attention to their children through what she describes as 'play listening'.

Many children learn that they can only reliably get an adult's attention by behaving badly or doing something that irritates the adult. The quality of attention that they receive at this point is usually poor but, to the child, must seem preferable to no attention at all. To be ignored is the worst punishment; it does seem that for more desperate children this feeling may be more extreme and they may feel that they only exist or that they only matter when they are being 'noticed'. In the absence of positive emotional interactions, an interaction filled with negative emotion can be needed to provide this sense of being real or alive.

Because this type of response fails in actually meeting the child's needs, the behaviour is repeated in the 'hope' that 'this time it will work' – like any addiction, it is only a temporary fix. The behaviour will not only be repeated when the child is reminded of those particular feelings but also when the child perceives an adult as 'likely to provide the attention they seek'. This may explain why a 'businesslike' teacher may be treated better by pupils than a 'caring' one. The most effective teachers are likely to be those who are able to adjust their 'style' to the requirements of the situation.

John Robertson in his training sessions and in Robertson (1989) highlights the importance of how we appear as teachers to the pupil in the process of gaining their co-operation. Where the teacher's own feelings guide the interaction, communication is often unsuccessful, especially in the longer term. Where the teacher takes into account 'the receptive state' of the pupil and adjusts their choice of words, tone of voice, expression, posture and proximity appropriately, then a successful interaction is more likely. Bill Rogers points out that both teacher and pupil can sometimes benefit from a period of cooling off following an emotional interaction.

'If you carry on like that it will end in tears...'

Many parents are familiar with the experience of their young children behaving badly towards bedtime. This frequently leads to an 'accident' that ends in tears or in some kind of confrontation with the parent. Often, a firmly but lovingly expressed 'No!' will be adequate to unlock the gates of emotion.

It is as if the child recognises that in order to be able to calm down to go to sleep they need to release some of the pent-up feelings that they have gathered during the day. Where this fails to happen adequately or effectively (often because the parent lacks time or is stressed themselves) the child is left with a backlog of unexpressed feelings. This can leave them in a whinging or whining mode or alternatively the feelings may temporarily disappear only to re-emerge when a similar situation arises at some future point. The child then continues to behave 'badly' in order to elicit a response from the parent that will help them release the residue of feelings through for instance, crying, tantrums and laughter. If this continues, the child may then turn to other 'caring' adults such as teachers for the attention they crave.

When I was a teacher in an off-site unit for pupils with behavioural difficulties, one of them turned up one afternoon with a large piece of wood. It required the intervention of the police and a police cell to be able to provide the firmness that he needed to stop. The older and bigger children get, the harder it is to provide firm limits which reinforces the importance of intervention in Reception and KS1 wherever possible.

Teachers can be inadvertently drawn into responding to the behaviour rather than (at least in part) to the need being expressed by the child through the behaviour. This can lead to an exacerbation of the behaviour difficulties. Dreikurs (1982) discusses an approach to responding to the underlying feeling which he describes as 'revealing the pupil's mistaken goal'. In order to minimise the child's confusion between 'what is OK at home and what is OK at school', school structures and routines need to emphasise the differences so that the child's hopes of gaining the kind of attention that they are not receiving at home are not unwittingly encouraged.

What also needs to be emphasised is that the school has other things to offer, such as opportunities for success in learning and the development of positive relationships with peers and adults. It may also be necessary for the school to identify strategies involving outside agencies through the development of Pastoral Support Plans.

'Containing' feelings in school

Behaviour policies and structures that create safety through emphasising clarity, consistency and fairness, and that focus on the positive and raise their pupils' self-esteem, are likely to minimise behaviour difficulties. Such policies help make it clear that a school is unable to meet these 'frozen needs' from the child's past, but that they are able to meet some of the real needs that the child has. If schools can provide a positive ethos and environment in which the pupil

- is physically and emotionally safe,

- can experience that they belong and are valued,

- can have successful learning experiences and grow in confidence and competence,

then the school can feel that they have done much to minimise the factors that can trigger difficult behaviour as well as maximising the growth of pupils that are confident, resilient, resourceful and have a zest for learning. Schools are not responsible for sorting pupils' feelings out but they can provide a combination of warm relationships and clear discipline structures which may then enable pupils to feel safe enough to learn to contain their own feelings and make the best of the learning opportunities on offer.

Feelings and emotions as triggers for behaviour difficulties

Table 6.1 indicates a range of feelings that can arise within the school situation. Column 2 suggests behaviours, which might result, and column 3 suggests broad strategies for minimising the inadvertent triggering of such feelings. It is important to remember that the emotional content of our communication through choice of words, tone of voice, posture and body language can be more important than the strategy itself. Strategies that emphasise all the familiar concepts such as creating consistency, predictability and safety, communication of respect, enhancing self-esteem and independence are important, but it is important to remember that there are no right or foolproof ways of doing these things and creativity is of the essence.

Table 6.1 Feelings, behaviours and strategies

Feeling	Possible behaviour	Strategies to minimise or avoid inappropriate behaviour
Frustrated/stupid	Temper outbursts; playing the class clown; behaviour that distracts away from the work or getting sent out; destroying own or other's work; poor quality work; inability to cope with challenge; new work	Appropriate tasks and subtasks; appropriate and relatively immediate positive feedback; being prepared for the task – work set in a context ('This is what we're going to do, these are the words we will use, this is what I want you to do, this is how it will look, these are the steps you will take – here they are written down'); reflection: 'Oh, what a shame. You must feel really fed-up that the model fell down again.'
Angry	'Make me' behaviour – refusal to co-operate or work; temper outbursts	Acknowledging the pupil's feeling; self-monitoring of feelings; temper control groups
Anxious or scared	Over-reaction or 'stupid'/unresponsive; silly behaviour; laughing or smiling; 'Not waving but drowning'; frozen or frozen grin; aggressive behaviour; 'Make me' behaviour; constant need for reassurance; daydreaming; deliberate destructive behaviour; 'provocative victim'	Clear rules; routines – predictable and consistent responses; clear signs that things are safe – teacher 'in control', e.g. incidents seen to be acted on; activities preparing for transition (yr 1–2, yr 6–7)
Lonely	Isolation; 'lost'; always on the periphery; last one to be chosen	Being noticed appropriately; tasks which involve joining in; hearing about others; working with others; circle time – co-operative activities; sharing experiences – role playing; making friends; being taught playground games (they could then teach them); setting up lunchtime clubs/activities
Not mattering, insignificant	Bully; victim; provocative	Being noticed, having appropriate attention, finding reasons why you matter; status – board monitor; team work
Out of place, confused	Always getting it wrong, no sense of routine or rules; isolated; not included	Explicit and consistent rules, routines and expectations; predictable responses to positive and negative behaviour; disapproving of the behaviour not the child; rehearsal of making friends; circle of friends; encouraging workmates; roles; status positions; activities
Miserable, depressed	Withdrawn; little or no enthusiasm; difficulty finishing work	Interesting work; pleasant activities; opportunities to talk; verbal acknowledgement of unhappiness; involvement with others; positive feedback
Disappointed, let down, betrayed, blamed	Blaming others – always their fault; unreliable; little trust	Clear and agreed behaviour and work expectations and limits; agreed picture of what 'it looks like when it's right'; follow-up to show you are consistent and trustworthy; fair treatment
Embarrassed	Lying; laughing; smirking (particularly when confronted); changing subject	Where possible avoid overwhelming attention; opportunities to have practice at dealing with attention – e.g. circle time
Overwhelmed	Apparent disinterest; defensive	Appropriate demands to build confidence at task; pupil involved in incremental plan for tasks; 'Solution-focused Brief Therapy' strategies
Bored	Dreaming; disruptive activities; activities that create 'entertainment'	Appropriate, meaningful and stimulating challenges and tasks

Schooling and Maslow's hierarchy of needs

Maslow's Hierarchy of Needs
Self-actualisation
Self-esteem
Social needs
Survival and Safety needs
Physiological

Note: This has been modified by shifting the 'Survival' aspect up a level and combining it with 'Safety' needs.

Maslow's 'hierarchy of needs' postulates that a person must have their needs met at one stage before moving on to the next. For instance, a pupil cannot be fully involved in the learning process in school while they are hungry or feeling scared or badly about themselves. In order for schools to create an effective learning environment these needs should be acknowledged and responded to appropriately.

Some needs can be met while others cannot be. For instance, a school should attempt to make itself a safe place for all pupils. However, a pupil who is being abused at home may well not *feel safe* in school because of the feelings that they bring from home. It makes sense for the school to recognise that this situation may well affect the pupil's ability to learn but it is also important to identify areas of school life that may remind the child of those feelings and, if possible, modify the situation to minimise their effects.

Physiological/survival need: food and drink

The need to survive is fundamental. For some children, these basic needs are not consistently met within the family situation and they can arrive at school without adequate food or sleep. While children are hungry they are unlikely to be able to engage completely with academic tasks presented. Some schools have dealt with this problem by providing breakfast clubs or by individual teachers having a supply of biscuits for particularly needy individuals.

At a broader level, late morning can often be a difficult time in terms of behaviour management. As children's blood-sugar levels drop it becomes physically harder for them to concentrate. Due to the timing of lunchtimes within the school day, some children, and in the end staff, can be put at a great disadvantage.

Dietary issues that may need to be considered by schools might include the eating of sweets or drinks with a high sugar content as these can drastically affect a child's blood-sugar balance with a consequent effect on attention and behaviour. Caffeine-containing drinks such as some colas may contribute to difficulties. Certain additives and colourings are also believed by some authorities to do this.

The need for safety

Pupils need to feel safe from physical or emotional threat in order to feel free to turn their attention to other matters such as learning and co-operating with others. Such threats may stem from circumstances in the home (physical, emotional or sexual abuse) or be present in school (perhaps bullying). The events may be current or they may be in the past but still be casting a powerful shadow into the present. When children feel under threat they are likely to feel that they have to protect themselves by acting out or withdrawing. When children have been sensitised in this way they may not be able to distinguish between real and imagined threats and so over-react to essentially inoffensive situations.

Another way to view such reactions is to see them as the child finding a moderately 'safe' situation to express similar but deeper emotions. This sort of dynamic also explains why people go to the cinema to feel scared or have a good cry or when a child leaves a party and sobs inconsolably when their balloon bursts. Simply, these events become opportunities for an individual to deal with much larger emotional issues in safe, bite-sized chunks. When dealing with such situations it is important to respond to the emotion that the individual is experiencing whether we are able to recognise its significance or not.

Home experiences

Often, troublesome children come from backgrounds:

- that lack clear, consistent and predictable limits;

- that have a lack of warmth, positive feedback or valuing of the child for themselves, or where such occurrences are unpredictable or inconsistent;

- where reactions/responses to children are based on adults' feelings (not even necessarily about the child) rather than respect, logic or rationality;

- where children are either left unsupervised or always have to fit in with the needs of adults;

- where children are given attention only when they demand it, often inappropriately;

- that are not safe either because of direct abuse or exposure to inappropriate sights or experiences;

- where children are treated as *bad* when they *behave* badly;

- where children have few opportunities to spend time with adults giving them full, interested attention, showing them in Rogers' words, 'unconditional positive regard' particularly while they are playing/learning;

- where there is an absence of modelling of appropriate ways to manage one's own feelings. Often – '*Do as I tell you*' rather than '*Do as I do*'. *How to Talk So Kids Will Listen and How to Listen So Kids Will Talk* (Faber and Mazlish, 1980) is a useful book for parents and teachers of younger pupils.)

A child is more likely to feel safe in school:

- where the adults seem confident and in control;

- when there are clear rules/expectations which are consistently enforced;

- where there are logical consequences to misbehaviour;

- when responses to good and bad behaviour are predictable and fair;

- when limits are known and are not dependent on a teacher's particular level of tolerance on a particular day;

- where the atmosphere is positive and encouraging;

- where incidents that do occur are seen to be dealt with;

- where children's concerns are listened to;

- where repetitive transgressions are dealt with more seriously and the pupil does not feel that things just 'go back to square one' after each incident;

- where they have positive peer relationships;

- where instances of good behaviour and work are identified more frequently than poor work and behaviour (Alistair Smith in his presentations has recommended a ratio of 4 positives to 1 negative; his book (Smith, 1996) is extremely stimulating and contains a wide range of ideas and approaches for raising self-esteem and pupil achievement);

- where pupils are not forced into situations that they cannot handle. Playtimes that are a time of minimal structure and supervision are often the worst situation for some children to manage. They then seem forced to behave badly in order to be brought in to avoid it. Schools need to address issues such as this. At other times, pupils cannot cope with classroom situations. Some schools have found it helpful to provide a 'storm home' (see Clarke and Murray, 1996) where they can go before something happens, until such time as they can manage.

Cues and communication in behaviour management

In creating safety for pupils, it is important to develop a stepped approach so that we are able to respond to behaviour with the minimum of disruption to the teaching and learning process. Rogers (1990c) refers to such a set of strategies as LIMI (Least Intrusive to Most Intrusive), the intention being to identify the least intrusive strategy that will work in a situation. An important element of a stepped approach is to communicate the level of the problem to the pupil so that they can adjust their behaviour accordingly. Such a cueing and warning system is particularly important for children who come from chaotic or inconsistent backgrounds. For children who have a poor understanding of social conventions, these will need to be taught.

Disruptive behaviour can be seen as an attempt on the part of the pupil to establish boundaries or to have them enforced – so that they can feel safe. Once they feel secure, they are then able to put their attention on the task at hand. Sometimes schools expect the putting in place of a structure to magically prevent a difficult pupil from making further transgressions. Unfortunately, it may be necessary for the most desperate pupils to experience the full range of sanctions before they understand that the staff will be consistent; the pupil will then be more likely to respond to strategies lower down the hierarchy. Good behaviour management is unlikely to eliminate bad behaviour; what it does aim to do is to lessen the likelihood of it happening, minimise its severity when it does occur and maximise the chance of a rapid return to the task-in-hand with relationships repaired, once it has stopped.

Social needs – the need to be cared about and to belong

Maslow, Dreikurs and others have identified the need of children to have a sense of belonging. The rituals and routines of school such as register-taking, assembly, team sports and even whole-class teaching can provide opportunities for this. Group differences as well as individual differences can make it difficult for some children to feel as if they belong. Broad factors that might prevent pupils feeling as if they don't belong might include physical differences, physical disabilities, race and ethnicity, mobility and poverty. Two further areas are gender and class.

Gender

Experience suggests that the majority of referrals to special needs services, whether for learning or behaviour, are boys. This might indicate a difficulty for many boys in 'fitting in' with the school organisation and resources. For many boys, just to be in a classroom doing ordinary school work can be quite an effort and many cannot wait to be out in the playground playing football. The value placed on academic activities by the school is frequently much higher than that placed on the kinds of activities that some boys might be more interested in. This may suggest reasons why boys often dominate both classroom and playground. It may be interesting to view the difficulty not as 'a problem with boys' but as an indication that some of their basic needs are not being met by current educational provision.

Class

The values promoted in schools usually relate strongly to academic success. These values are traditionally more likely to be held by middle-class families in this country. Schools may therefore favour middle-class children because they are most suited to pupils who live in homes where:

- education is valued as an end in itself;
- the parents have had good experiences of schooling and regard education positively;
- the parents feel confident and comfortable with schools as organisations and teachers as professionals;
- books are freely available and reading is valued;
- support and resources for homework are freely available;
- family mobility is not an issue;
- the cost of uniform, equipment and trips etc. is not a problem;
- parents can effectively contribute to homework or broader aspects of school life.

Excluded pupils

A particular group of pupils who find it difficult to feel that they belong are those who are excluded as a result of their behaviour and either have to return to their own school or have to transfer to another. Some schools recognise that it is important to be proactive by making particular efforts to reintegrate these pupils by providing a range of 'positive engagement' strategies to facilitate this process.

Transition time

Another crucial time to focus on 'belonging' is when pupils transfer from one school to another (or indeed from one class to another). Strong feelings of fear and anxiety as well as of hope and expectation can be evoked by this aspect of school life which, if not well managed, can lead to difficulties in adjustment. Some schools provide opportunities for visits or set up joint projects; these are likely to be most effective where there are opportunities for the pupils to articulate their feelings about the changes. It is easier for pupils to move on and embrace the new situation if the sadness and loss, fear and anxiety are acknowledged. Such work can happen directly through activities such as circle time or more indirectly through writing, drama or 'research projects'.

School strategies

In order to create a sense of 'belonging', there needs to be a perception of what the school stands for and the values that it holds, particularly in relation to its pupils. A school can do this by highlighting:

• how members of 'this school' do things;

• what 'this school' is proud about;

• how we show off our school and ourselves;

This can be achieved by:

• the way the school looks inside and presents itself to the outside world;

• the way staff are seen to treat one another;

• the way staff are seen to treat pupils;

• the way all members of the school treat parents and visitors;

• the displays on the walls (research by Professor Harry Daniels *et al.* has revealed interesting information about how pupils perceive displays of their work and of the values that they transmit, e.g. do the displays value conformity or diversity? Smith (1996) argues that it is preferable to put information relating to current topics and work on the walls rather than pupils' work);

• weekly 'positive feedback' assemblies;

• where pupils excluded from class are placed, e.g. not in the entrance hall;

• successes appearing in the local media.

Many of these ideas can be directly translated to the classroom.

Classroom strategies

These include the following:

• co-operative activities and team games to strengthen group identity;

• 'following instruction' games such as Simon Says in order to develop positive experiences of co-operating and following instructions;

• developing 'our class rules';

• bringing in 'visitors' or outsiders;

• circle-time activities such as: 'Sharing things we have in common' or 'silent statements' (these allow people to acknowledge the truth of a statement for them, e.g., 'All those wearing blue socks stand up and change places'; 'All those who have experienced bullying in this school, stand up and change places'; this process is shown in the 'Lucky Duck' Circle Time video (see the Videos section in the Bibliography));

- special roles and other ways to contribute to the class/school;
- 'friendship trees';
- exploring developing friendships through role-play;
- ensuring that rules and routines are clearly understood; many rules are unspoken and children from differing cultures and backgrounds may benefit from these being made explicit so that a common understanding of them can be established;
- practising conflict resolution strategies/assertiveness strategies for dealing with difficult situations.

Although these strategies can be used to improve particular individuals' difficulties, many of them can be used to deal with whole classes if, for instance, they have a problem 'gelling'/being able listen to one another/following instructions.

It is interesting to note that one of the points from the summary of *Bright Futures* (Mental Health Foundation, 1999) identifies an increase in problems in the area of interpersonal skills:

> Fear of abuse and fears about road safety together with a reduction in neighbour and extended family responsibility for the community's children are increasing the number of children who are unpractised in making and consolidating friendships, dealing with conflict, taking risks and team games – all key components of emotional literacy.

A key skill is not so much giving attention to children but identifying what can simply be done to make them feel noticed, e.g. using their name, noticing something about them, referring to something they have said previously, commenting on their football team, allowing them to overhear you positively commenting to a colleague about their behaviour or work.

Belonging involves not only being noticed and being valued but also being able to contribute to the group through, perhaps, special roles or opportunities to contribute to class discussion. For particularly isolated pupils 'Circles of Friends' (a strategy for involving members of a class in supporting an individual child who may be isolated – see 'Circles of friends' in *Educational Psychology in Practice* **11** (4) (1996)) can be a positive experience for both the individual and the class.

Perhaps the most powerful tool that a school has in terms of behaviour management is for pupils to have a sense that they have something to lose by jeopardising their relationship with the school. Once a pupil feels that they have nothing to lose, the task becomes much harder. It can be productive to make it clear to pupils whose behaviour stems from a difficult home background that they have a choice about whether they wish to create in school similar difficulties to home or whether they wish to make school a haven from those difficulties.

Lee Cantor, famous for the 'assertive discipline' approach to behaviour management, in a recent presentation (Birmingham, 1998) was emphasising the importance of building positive relationships with pupils with behaviour difficulties and that without this basis, many behaviour strategies would have limited effect. Strategies such as star charts may work at a behaviour modification level but they can often be most effective when used as a means for teachers to reinforce a warm, positive relationship.

It is important to recognise that the ability to fit in to school life is not a definer of quality of the individual or an accurate predictor of their ability to make a success of their lives outside the narrow confines of the school system. Schools may have to say that it is not possible to contain a particular pupil within the system as it exists, but should hold on to the idea that the pupil is not inherently bad or inadequate for being unable to function within it.

Self-esteem

> Whatever we show to other people, we always get a backstage view of ourselves.
> (Garrison Keillor)

Self-esteem (or positive self-regard as Rogers termed it) is built from the responses of those around a child and is the difference between their actual self and their ideal self. As Fontana (1993) puts it, 'Self-esteem is concerned with the value we place on ourselves...', that is, the difference between how the pupil has learned to perceive themselves and how they believe they ought to be.

The initial influence on a child will be the parents or carers, but as the child grows older, peers and other adults make their contribution. At a broader level, the societal groups of class, race and gender with which the individual identifies can also affect an individual's self-esteem.

Fontana (1993) in discussing Coopersmith's (1967) work identifies the following home factors in the development of high self-esteem:

- respect was shown for their opinions and points of view;

- parents knew a great deal about their children and showed interest in them;

- parents showed affection to their children;

- there was consistency in the use of discipline;

- discipline relied upon rewards for good behaviour and upon withdrawal of approval for bad.

Societal patterns of racism, classism and sexism can be mirrored or minimised by the values and practices adopted by schools. These can, in turn, affect the way these factors affect individual pupils and their response to the demands of the education system. Schools that recognise these dynamics are likely to respond positively and be proactive in dealing with these issues. A sense of being valued is a vital ingredient in developing trust between pupils and their teachers as well as between parents and the school.

Identifying self-esteem

Table 6.2 indicates some of the characteristics of pupils with high and low self-esteem. From the table, it can be seen that many of the qualities that are hoped for in a pupil are related to high self-esteem and that many behaviours which are of concern to teachers are associated with low self-esteem.

Lawrence (1987) has discussed how giving pupils regular counselling from non-professionals not only raised self-esteem but also improved their reading skills. It would be unusual now for schools to be able to find those levels of human resource or time. Nevertheless, one headteacher identified a particular skill of effective teachers as 'communicating that they are paying attention to pupils when they listen to them, even for very brief interactions'. Ted Wragg in a recent talk to headteachers (Leeds, October 1999), reported some research which suggested that teachers have

Table 6.2 Characteristics of pupils with high and low self-esteem

High self-esteem	Low self-esteem
Confident/assured/self-reliant	Lack confidence or anxious; need to please; over-react to situations
Independent learner	Continual need for reassurance/guidance
Stand up for themselves	Get teased, bullied or ignored
Can show initiative and leadership	Over-assertive; aggressive; need to dominate others
Can take responsibility for their behaviour	Full of excuses for behaviour; blame others; feel that they are unfairly treated
Work/play well with others	Isolated or unpopular
Listen well to peers and adults	No attention for others
Generally appropriate and co-operative behaviour	Attention seeking; reassurance seeking
Others listen to them	Ignored
Can cope with frustration	React badly to frustration
Can learn from failure	Easily give up; destroy work; feel stupid
Accept appropriate criticism	Overwhelmed by criticism; ignore/deny criticism
Realistic view of themselves and their abilities	Unrealistic views of themselves and their abilities
Gain attention appropriately	Gain attention inappropriately; class clown or need to impress others
Able to respond flexibility and deal with changes	Lack of flexibility and inability to deal with disappointment
Able to work at tasks	Distract attention away from work
Able to read/respond to social signals	Inability to read social signals
Emotions – a response to the present	Emotions dominated by past events

more than a thousand pupil interactions on a daily basis, which, as he points out, is one reason why teaching is such hard work. What it also means is that there are many possibilities each day for enhancing individual pupils' self-esteem if the quality, rather than the length, of the interaction is considered.

Solution-focused brief therapy (see Durrant, 1995) is a fairly recent approach to counselling which is sometimes used by educational psychologists. It combines a number of strategies that can also be applied less formally in the classroom by teachers. These include approaches that:

- focus on an individual's successes – 'When did it work?', 'Which bits did go right?', 'When didn't the problem occur?';

- break down the gap between self-concept and ideal self into manageable steps for planned change – encouraging the pupil themselves to identify the next step for change.

The importance of setting small targets in order to make goals manageable is also focused on by educationalists such as Clarke (1998) where she discusses how important it is to involve the pupils as fully as possible in this process. The possibility of increasing pupils' sense of competence and confidence through this kind of process is central to the demands of the classroom today.

Strategies for raising self-esteem include:

- creating opportunities for success;

- minimising the possibility of failure or 'getting it wrong';

- identifying 'the bits that did work', the times 'it didn't go wrong';

- reminding pupils of their past successes;

- strategies from other perspectives such as: 'reframing' and structured reward programmes (although I dislike the use of the term 'reward': concrete positive reinforcement or feedback are more accurate and avoid some of the difficulties associated with the word reward), SMART (Specific, Measurable, Achievable, Relevant, Time-limited) targets;

- creating realistic choices;

- managing behaviour through focusing on the work;

- regular and frequent-enough positive feedback; some pupils require it once a day; others (initially at least) several times an hour;

- circle time.

Not waving but drowning

> I was much too far out all my life and not waving but drowning.
>
> (Stevie Smith, 'Not Waving But Drowning')

A number of pupils with low self-esteem hide their feelings or compensate for them by attention-seeking or aggressive strategies. (Also included in this group are those pupils who are always out of their seat, frequently causing disruption and who make little or no eye-contact. They are sometimes defined as having ADHD but equally the behaviour can result from the child not feeling 'contained' by existing boundaries and is often caused by anxiety and fear.)

Adults' reactions can be unhelpful by responding to external behaviour rather than recognising the internal need being expressed. We can mistakenly believe that in some way they are enjoying themselves rather than showing their desperation. By communicating to the pupil through everyday interactions that you see the underlying feelings that are bothering them they may be less driven to behaviours aimed at letting you know how they feel: 'You're looking fed-up, are things not going well at home?' or 'You must feel very fed-up about that piece of work. I bet you feel like throwing it away, but actually there are a number of good things about it.'

Self-actualisation

> If you can trust yourself when all men doubt you
> And make allowance for their doubting too
>
> (Kipling, 'If')

In school, this stage is concerned with becoming an individual and an independent learner. (Stephen Covey (Covey, 1992) has developed a three-level model of dependence/independence/interdependence which is relevant to this section.) Self-actualisation in school may involve taking a step forward in academic learning but might equally happen outside of that structure, perhaps performing in a school production or achieving in sport. Many pupils can attain significant successes outside of school, for instance, in the arts; some young people can earn considerable amounts of money through activities such as modelling. It can be salutary for teachers to recognise that their pupils can, in some ways, be more competent than themselves.

There are also other children who, because of lack of support at home and having to manage in very hostile situations, can become extremely streetwise. It cannot be easy for these pupils to fit in to some of the conforming aspects of school organisation as they may perceive that the school is not necessarily to be trusted and that their survival depends on their own self-reliance.

As well as the recognition of these kinds of competencies there also needs to be an acknowledgement that contemporary society does not allow young people, particularly adolescents, many real challenges. It is a natural desire of adolescents to test themselves out and, if legitimate opportunities are not available, then over-involvement in cyber-challenges, chemical experimentation or even anti-social and criminal activity will be more likely.

Teachers have feelings too...

The teacher with high self-esteem is likely to produce students with high self-esteem and also the converse.

(Lawrence, 1987)

It seems important at this point to recognise the fact that teachers are human beings and as such have feelings too. Behaviour can challenge teachers at a personal/emotional level as well as at a professional level. This is why dealing with it can be so difficult and even upsetting. Dreikurs (1982) discusses how teachers can use the feelings triggered by their interaction with a pupil to help identify appropriate strategies for managing them. He suggests one way to distinguish between attention-seeking behaviour, power-seeking behaviour and revenge-seeking behaviour is that in the first, the teacher is likely to feel irritated or annoyed. In the second, the teacher may well feel threatened or challenged. In the third, the teacher may feel defeated or hurt. These distinctions are important because he suggests different responses to the different levels of behaviour problem.

Teachers' feelings in such situations usually arise from their own unresolved issues (by the time the child reaches secondary age, threats might actually be real) and this means that they do not necessarily find it easy to remain objective about the pupil's behaviour. The teacher's immediate reaction may well be defensive which is unlikely to resolve the situation satisfactorily, leaving the teacher and the pupil feeling rather the worse for wear. The teacher's ability to manage such situations effectively depends on a number of factors including the procedures/structures that are in place as well as their confidence in the support that they might receive from colleagues.

The raising of self-esteem has been emphasised as central to positive strategies for encouraging good behaviour. Teachers whose own self-esteem is low will find it exceedingly difficult to execute strategies for pupils in this area. The morale of individuals as well as the school as a whole can play a vital role in the overall management of behaviour. As Lawrence has written:

In addition to the qualities of empathy, acceptance and genuineness [...], it seems that teachers who are able to delegate routine jobs, are able to find time to relate personally to the students, are tolerant of students' conversations, are generally relaxed in their teaching are those who also have high self-esteem. This implies they are able to present a high self-esteem model with which the students identify.

Effective teachers are able to distinguish between the acting out of their own feelings and using the expression of feelings as an effective means of communicating the severity of a problem to a pupil. It may be appropriate for a teacher to communicate how they feel through tone of voice and body language. This is consistent with Rogers' notions of empathy and congruency. In order to express feelings to emphasise a point, there must be no sense of the teacher 'losing it'. Failure to do this will only communicate to the pupil that the teacher (who should be in control of their feelings) is not. This can be alarming/entertaining to the pupil as well as being a poor model. When a teacher 'loses it' it means that their actions are driven by their own feelings rather than by whether their actions are having a desirable effect upon the child. Robertson (1989) discusses the problem of 'overdwelling' and the way in which it can make a pupil respond badly to reprimand rather than seeing it as appropriate. The skill of the teacher to bounce back to 'normal service' once a situation has been dealt with and not to hold on to (or at least communicate) their feeling of irritation and resentment is important but not necessarily easy.

There is a story that reflects this difference. It tells of a man walking along a road in India who observed a holy man removing a scorpion from a puddle in which it was drowning. The scorpion stung the priest whereupon it fell back in the puddle. This happened a number of times before the observer spoke to the priest and asked him why he continued to try to help the scorpion. The holy man replied, 'It is in the scorpion's nature to sting and it is in my nature to be compassionate.'

Endthought

This perspective has emphasised the importance of the way feelings motivate and guide pupils' behaviour. It has also tried to indicate how at least trying to hypothesise which feelings are involved in a situation may allow teachers to identify more effective strategies and modes of communication when dealing with behaviour difficulties.

While bearing in mind the ideas contained in this perspective, it is important for teachers to realise that it is not in their job description to be counsellors. It is, however, appropriate and desirable for teachers to be creative and imaginative in identifying opportunities to apply some of these ideas within their day-to-day teaching. Because of this, teachers are unlikely to have the time for the use of formal assessment instruments (e.g. Lawseq questionnaires, Denis Lawrence; Q-sort, Rogers; Repertory Grid Technique, Kelly).

More important may be the use of classroom observation. This can reveal the stage of the lesson that the pupil finds most difficult, e.g. class teaching, starting work, or continuing the task. It can also show whether behaviour difficulties are triggered by interactions with the teacher or with particular pupils. Many of the things (maybe choice of words, tone of voice etc.) that can provoke a reaction in pupils with low-self esteem are, for most pupils, unremarkable and need an outside pair of eyes to identify them.

Teachers' greatest resource is themselves which not only makes the job very rewarding but also is (partly) responsible, for it being so tiring.

7 The ecosystemic perspective

The ecosystemic model

This approach to behaviour is based on Systems theory and Family therapy. Molnar and Lindquist (1989) have applied the ecosystemic model to schools and classrooms. Such an approach regards school behaviour and classroom behaviour as having a reciprocal influence. Problem behaviours influence other behaviours. Perceptions of behaviours may influence problem behaviours. People's perceptions of interactions also influence behaviour. Essentially it involves looking at the different systems people are part of and the mutual influence of those systems. Emphasis is therefore placed on the contexts of behaviour and the influence of those contexts on behaviour. Behavioural change occurs through focusing on the context as well as the individual.

Systems theory

Systems theory (Bertalanffy, 1968) would see a school as being a system and as interconnected to other systems. Changes in one system will have an effect on other systems, e.g. changes in family systems can impact on school systems and changes in school systems can impact on family systems. Changes in parts of the system (subsystems) can affect other parts of the system, e.g. a change in the pastoral system of the school can impact on classroom behaviour and classroom behaviour can impact on the pastoral system. This circular action and reaction of systems is an example of recursive causality where systems and subsystems influence each other, a mutuality of influence. Interactions between members of systems and subsystems can be seen as reciprocal, that is influencing or disturbing each other.

Family therapy

Family therapy can be seen as an application of systems theory. Generally family therapy see families as systems. Problem behaviours are seen as being problems of the family as a whole. There are different schools of family therapy, e.g. the *Structural school* (Minuchin, 1974), the *Milan school* (Selvini-Palazzoli *et. al.*, 1974) and the *Strategic school* (Haley, 1970)

The Milan Systemic school concentrates on how family members perceive and interpret events and aims to uncover the influences that keep the family functioning in the way it does. Family members are seen as engaging in problem behaviours in order to maintain the family's equilibrium. It introduced paradoxical interventions, e.g. positive connotation and reframing.

The Structural school focuses on the problem context rather than the individual. It sees the family as going through a life-cycle or stages and emphasises power relationships and hierarchies within the family. Problems arise through family interactions. Families may be unable to cope with transitions and experience boundary problems, e.g. disengagement and enmeshment.

The Strategic school focuses on communications, the perceptions and belief systems within the family. Problems arise through faulty communication between family members particularly in terms of feelings or emotions.

Family therapy on the whole sees people as relating and interacting with one another in the family context through a desire for recognition and belonging. Families also relate to other systems. Through their actions or behaviour family members maintain the family as a system but in doing so they may suffer adverse consequences. For example, parents may displace family conflict on to a particular child. If the child has behaviour problems in the school the parents may see this as confirming their opinion of the child and respond negatively. The parents' reaction helps to preserve their relationship at the expense of one of their children. The school when informed of the parents' reaction in turn feels justified in their treatment of the child. Another example is where teachers displace their feelings of incompetence in classroom management on to a particular misbehaving child and locate in that child the reason for classroom disruption.

The family therapy approach seeks to understand relationships and problems within the family as functional or as arising through cycles of interactions between family members. Through these interactions, roles and boundaries are formed, behaviours encouraged or suppressed. The family therapy approach has also been applied to the school system in the sense of seeing the school as part of a *triangular relationship* between the family, child and school. For example, parents may come to value their child's problem behaviour in school as a way of displacing on to the school the negative feelings they have in their relationship. Another example would be where children displace negative feelings from their parents on to particular teachers who reprimand them.

The aim of family therapy is to change the negative cycle or dysfunctional interactions between family members without blaming or scapegoating particular members. The therapist intervenes at crucial points during the cycles of negative interactions. Family members' interactions are seen as resulting from circular causality not individual causation. Interventions therefore focus on interactions not individuals as such.

The ecosystemic approach to behaviour

This approach considers behaviour problems to be the product of interactions between teachers and students and between the students themselves. These interactions occur in certain contexts, e.g. classrooms, and should be understood as being a function of the specific context. Teachers and students engage in cycles of interactions that can be positive or negative. These interactions are seen as being the effects of *circular causality*, i.e. teachers and students contribute to and maintain particular patterns of interactions.

From this perspective it is important to consider the possible influence of wider systems and to look at problems in terms of different levels of analysis. At the *first level of analysis* behaviour problems will be seen as resulting from particular interactions that are occurring in the here-and-now, e.g. in classrooms. This level of analysis is facilitated through using the ABC or functional analysis. At the *second level the analysis* is widened to include the influences of other systems on classroom systems, e.g. how families impact on classroom systems, how classroom systems impact on families and how pastoral systems impact on families and classes.

This approach also emphasises the interconnectedness of all events in terms of cycles of cause and effect. Behaviour problems are seen as resulting from a series of actions and reactions which although appearing as problems for teachers may be seen by students as a means of resolving their own difficulties. Students may continue to repeat inappropriate behaviours as a means of coping with their own problems, e.g. students may leave their seats to avoid feelings of embarrassment or humiliation in connection with set tasks. Teachers' attempts to confront students perpetuate conflicts because teachers fail to deal with problems as perceived by their students.

Changing behaviour from this perspective requires teachers to examine their interpretations of student behaviour and also their students' perceptions of behaviour. Changes in interpretations or perceptions can lead to changes in behaviour. Teachers who continue to pursue the same ineffective interventions need to consider their interpretations of interactions between themselves and their students.

This perspective sees interventions as needing to take into consideration the perceptions, interpretations and behaviours of all the parties involved with problem behaviours. In the school context teachers should reflect on their own interpretations and behaviour and how they may be contributing to behaviour problems. The aim of an ecosystemic approach is to defuse confrontation and terminate negative interactions through initiating positive interactions between teachers and students. This requires teachers to engage in non-judgemental, problem-solving analyses that avoid self-perpetuating cycles of negative interactions.

Ecosystemic assessment

Definition

This form of assessment requires teachers to examine their interpretations of their interactions with students, other teachers and parents. The focus will be on current interpretations and attributions in particular contexts (e.g. peer group, classroom, pastoral system and home).

Rationale

The reason for this form of assessment is that students can be positively or negatively influenced by the interpretations of their behaviours by teachers, parents and peers. Students' behaviours may vary according to those interpretations. The reactions of significant others and interactions with them (e.g. teachers, parents and peers) can affect student behaviour by increasing or decreasing its frequency and duration. Students may become 'locked-into' a vicious circle of negative interactions leading to deteriorating behaviour.

Often the focus of assessments is solely on the students themselves (e.g. child-deficit models) to the exclusion of other factors namely interactions with others. The exclusion of other factors may prevent the construction of more valid assessments of student behaviour. It is often necessary to look at teachers' beliefs, attitudes, expectations, attributions and inferences about students in order to assess student behaviour fully.

The process

The assessment process should include the collection of information about students, interactions with their various systems, e.g. teachers, parents and peers and their interpretations of their interactions. Assessment in the first instance will be based on undertaking analyses of the different kinds of interactions that occur within the classroom, in the school and between families and the school.

- *The classroom context*: interactions between teachers and students and students and their peers, e.g. teachers may see students as simply wanting to disrupt the lesson whereas students may be responding to what they see as teachers' indifference to their need for help with the work set.

- *The classroom–pastoral system context*: interactions between teachers, students and the pastoral system in the school. Teachers may frequently send students to headteachers or heads of year resulting in the pastoral system being overused or overloaded thus reducing the effectiveness of this type of intervention. In this case teachers come to regard the pastoral system as inadequate, pastoral staff regard teachers as incompetent at classroom management and the pastoral system ends up dealing inadequately with students' problems.

- *The family–school context*: interactions between families and the school. Teachers who regard parents as hostile to the school confront them with the problem behaviour of their children. The parents respond negatively, accusing teachers of victimisation. Teachers feel that their initial perceptions are correct. Students feel vindicated by their parents' accusations against teachers and continue their problem behaviour.

An analysis of the context will describe the interactions without attributing blame, searching for a definitive cause of the behaviour or locating the cause within a particular individual. An analysis of behaviour difficulties will include understanding how the participants perceive and interpret the behaviour of all those involved with the problem, in other words, the meanings they attribute to the behaviour giving cause for concern.

An example might be students who are continually out of seat and being reprimanded by teachers. Teachers may see the problem behaviour as simply disobedience and nothing more and also as completely unjustifiable. The student disciplined may perceive being out of seat as a means of avoiding work that is too difficult and therefore justifiable. Some students may see teachers as being unfair in ignoring the student's learning difficulties. Other students may see the student concerned as disrupting lessons and preventing them from working. The parents may see the teacher as being annoyed with their child because of the demands their child's learning difficulties place on the teacher's time. The teacher may see the parents as colluding with the child in order to excuse what the teacher regards as the parents' poor upbringing of their child.

Assessment procedures

Information should be collected on the following.

1. *specific contexts*:
   - the specific contexts where negative interactions occur (e.g. classroom, school and home);

- the locations where negative interactions appear and where they do not appear (e.g. with particular teachers and during particular lessons or activities);

2. *interpretations, attributions and expectations*: the interpretations, attributions and expectations that teachers have with respect to the student and those the student has with respect to teachers;

3. *interactions*: the positive and/or negative interactions between the student and significant others;

4. *skills*: the strengths and weaknesses the student possesses in terms of being able to enter into positive interactions with teachers and peers;

5. *analysis*:
   - using the accumulated information to arrive at an assessment that leads to a formulation in terms of how perceptions and interpretations influence and maintain the problem behaviour;
   - specific interventions that focus on changing the perceptions and interpretations of the problem behaviours in a way that leads to positive rather than negative interactions.

Specific techniques

Observation

Observations in the relevant context should be undertaken with the aim of describing interactions in objective terms. This can be achieved by using a Fixed Interval Sampling sheet, a Behaviour Frequency sheet and an ABC sheet. These sheets enable the observer to describe the antecedents, consequences, frequency and duration of the observed behaviours; see Ayers *et al.* (1996).

The perceptions of different participants or observers can be compared with the observations. The results can form the basis for ecosystemic interventions. For example observations may show that teachers' perceptions of student behaviour are inaccurate. Observational feedback to teachers could lead to positive changes in teachers' perceptions and behaviour.

Behaviour checklists and rating scales

These instruments enable teachers to rate students in terms of specific categories, e.g. the Primary and Secondary Assessment Profiles can be used to record and collate information about pupils' behaviours; see Resources section below and Ayers (1996).

Sociometry

This technique, largely devised by J.L. Moreno, is a means of discovering how far pupils are accepted by the peer group and the structure and relationships within the group. Students may be accepted, rejected or ignored. Sociograms could help teachers identify the dominant students, different sub-groups and students who are rejected or isolated. See for example Figure 7.1.

Self-reports can also be used to discover how students describe and value their interactions with others. Another method is the *Q-Sort procedure* (devised by W. Stephenson) when students 'sort out' from presented statements what they would

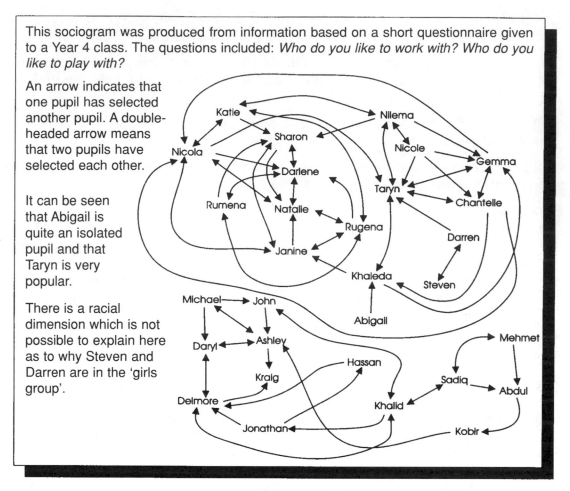

This sociogram was produced from information based on a short questionnaire given to a Year 4 class. The questions included: *Who do you like to work with? Who do you like to play with?*

An arrow indicates that one pupil has selected another pupil. A double-headed arrow means that two pupils have selected each other.

It can be seen that Abigail is quite an isolated pupil and that Taryn is very popular.

There is a racial dimension which is not possible to explain here as to why Steven and Darren are in the 'girls group'.

Figure 7.1 Example sociogram

like to be (the ideal self) and what they are (the actual self). Teachers compare the ideal and actual selves for discrepancies and consider the implications of discrepancies in terms of an intervention.

Ecosystemic formulation

An ecosystemic formulation sees problem behaviour as arising from negative interactions between teachers and students, between students, between teachers and parents and between parents and their children. Students' problem behaviours may arise through negative interactions in the following ways:

- students' perceptions of their teachers' actions (e.g. a student sees teachers as disliking him);

- students' perceptions of other students' behaviour (e.g. other students see the student as 'thick', the student feeling rejected becomes aggressive towards peers, ends up escalating into cycles of negative interactions);

- teachers' perceptions (e.g. seeing the student as simply malicious in disrupting lessons, as a result teacher does not consider alternative explanations);

- parents' perceptions (e.g. seeing their child as being victimised by teachers, as a result the student resists and challenges teachers' negative perceptions, this leads to an increase in negative interactions).

Students' behaviours are seen as due not only to the expression of within-child factors but also to teachers' perceptions. Problem behaviours arise through interactions between people embedded in different systems. In the example above student problems are seen as arising through interactions between teacher and parents, teacher and student and student and peers. Interactions need to be directed and focused on the interactions taking place between different systems. See the Analysis of Interactions Sheet in Figure 7.2 and a full version in the Resources section at the end of the book.

Ecosystemic interventions

These types of interventions are ones proposed by Molnar and Lindquist (1989) that draw on approaches in family therapy. These interventions are based on the *paradoxical techniques* in family therapy that are used to promote new interpretations and to allow different perspectives to develop alongside formerly entrenched viewpoints. Ecosystemic interventions are based on the idea that all participants through their interactions contribute in some way to problem behaviour. This approach asks all the parties to reflect on their perceptions of the problem behaviour. Teachers should critically examine their perceptions and interpretations of student behaviour. Through positive reinterpretations the cycles of negative reactions are hopefully terminated. The aim is to avoid confrontations between teachers and students that escalate into an ongoing series of self-perpetuating conflicts.

Teachers are asked to provide behavioural analyses of problem behaviours, e.g. specific and accurate descriptions of student behaviours, their contexts and the antecedents and consequences of those behaviours. Simultaneously teachers should provide their current interpretations of student behaviours.

Ecosystemic interventions occur when teachers use alternative interpretations to explain problem behaviour. The main aim is for teachers to apply positive interpretations that terminate negative cycles of escalation and confrontation. A positive interpretation is one that redefines the problem behaviour as one not of conflict but as one that is possibly serving a useful function within the interaction.

Sleuthing

Sleuthing is when teachers raise questions and look for clues in order to solve problem behaviour. Teachers should analyse their perceptions and interpretations of student behaviour, their students' interactions and expectations. The teachers' focus should be on identifying and encouraging positive changes in student behaviour. Teachers should also consider positive interpretations of problem behaviour in order to facilitate a new cycle of positive interactions that all parties can then perceive as a fresh start.

Reframing

This particular intervention is based on the idea that there are different, equally valid interpretations of the same behaviour or situations and that the behaviours of teachers and students will reflect those different interpretations. If interpretations change then

ANALYSIS OF INTERACTIONS SHEET

Name: *John Doe*   **Age:** *11*   **Date:** *1* | *1* | *94*

Form/Class *Form 7R*   **NC Year:** *7*

1) Describe how you perceive the interactions between yourself and the target pupil

in positive as well as negative terms

In negative terms: I see John as abusive and rude towards me in particularly when I ask him to do some work, pay attention or to stop shouting out to other pupils.

In positive terms: I find that John on the rare occasion will ask me to help him with his work and even thank me afterwards.

2) Describe how other staff perceive the target pupil

in positive as well as negative terms

In negative terms: Some teachers say he is just the same in their lessons, rude and abusive. These teachers take him for Maths and Science. I gather from them that he has difficulty with his work.

In positive terms: Some teachers say he is not a behaviour problem in their lessons and gets on with his work and is not rude to them. These teachers take him for practical subjects such as Art whereas I take him for French which he finds difficult.

3) Describe how you perceive the interactions between the target pupil and other pupils

in positive as well as negative terms

In negative terms: Some pupils dislike him because he interferes or distracts them from their work when he talks to them. He appears somewhat isolated. But others find him a laugh and would follow his lead if I didn't intervene.

In positive terms: One pupil sometimes helps him with his work and when this happens he tends to behave pleasantly to some of the other pupils as well.

4) Describe how you perceive the interactions within the target pupil's family and between the family and the school

John comes from a family which is hostile to the school and towards me in particular. He has brothers who have attended this school and who have had me as their French teacher. They have also been rude and abusive. The parents always appear to take the side of their children when they come up to school but also complain about their children's rudeness towards them at home.

Figure 7.2 Analysis of Interactions

5) Describe any comparisons you are able to make between any observations undertaken of the target pupil: does this comparison highlight discrepancies or agreements. If so, what implications does it have for your picture of the pupil?

John does get on better in practical subjects where he is not asked to do so much reading and writing and where he can use his hands. However, in other subjects like Science and Maths he is just the same as he is in French. I used to think that John was rude and abusive towards all the teachers but I found that he tends to be like that in lessons where he has learning difficulties even though the teachers have different personalities than mine. My picture then is of a pupil whose behaviour changes according to the subject he takes. His behaviour does not seem to relate to the personality of the teacher.

6) From the above information, summarise your perceptions and those of others and state your expectations of the target pupil

I see John as behaving acceptably in some lessons because he can cope with the work and finds the subject interesting but in other subjects like mine he finds the work too difficult and resents being asked to get on with his work. If I left him alone I probably wouldn't be abused but then he would distract others and I would have to intervene..

7) If possible, REFRAME those expectations in such a way that the target pupil's problem is redefined more positively. Describe your 'reframing'.

John is a pupil who experiences behavioural difficulties in the context of those lessons where his literacy and numeracy skills are found wanting. His behaviour can be positive in other lessons whatever the personality of the teacher. John can show a better side to his nature and I now recognize that, I probably need to make French more accessible and enjoyable for him by enabling him to use his practical skills, by sitting him with a peer tutor and by giving him more individual support. His misbehaviour may be his way of trying to bring this to my attention.

behaviours will change. Teachers should look for positive interpretations of problem behaviour, i.e. 'reframe' the behaviour. The new interpretation should be positive, plausible and accurately reflect the situation.

For example, if a student is out of seat the teacher may interpret it as simply defiance or alternatively as being due to the student having difficulty with the work and fearing failure. Based on the first interpretation the teacher will continue to reprimand the student who, if quiet, will still not be able to cope with the set task. However the teacher can place a positive interpretation on the behaviour in the sense of interpreting the behaviour as an appeal for help on the part of the student. If interpreted this way then the situation can be turned from being one of conflict to one of co-operation. The student will remain seated as the teacher now recognises the student's learning difficulty and responds appropriately thereby giving the student attention. Confrontation will cease as both the teacher and student agree that it is the student's learning difficulty that is producing the cycle of negative interactions and that it is this difficulty that needs solving.

Procedure for reframing

- identify negative interpretations and responses to problem behaviour;

- consider plausible, alternative, positive interpretations of the behaviour;

- based on a positive interpretation respond differently to the problem behaviour.

Positive connotation of motive

This particular intervention is based on the idea that a student's problem behaviour can be positively motivated. A student's out-of-seat behaviour may be for a number of reasons all probably unverifiable. Instead of the teacher construing the student's motive as inevitably a negative one the teacher should consider a plausible alternative. In considering a positive motive the teacher is in a better position to change the situation by responding differently. The student's out-of-seat behaviour can be positively construed as an appeal for help, i.e. the student is seeking information from other students. The teacher increases support for the student.

Positive connotation of function

This particular intervention is based on the idea that problem behaviour can be interpreted as serving a positive function for the teacher. For example a student's out-of-seat behaviour is construed as bringing to the teacher's attention the seating arrangements in the classroom. The teacher by noticing this positive function perceives the student as paradoxically assisting the teacher in reviewing his seating plan. The teacher revises his seating plan placing the student next to students who can help the student with work.

Symptom prescription

This particular intervention is based on the idea that students frequently act in the way they do for positive reasons related to their circumstances. Paradoxically the teacher asks for the problem behaviour to continue but in different circumstances.

This requires the teacher to identify plausible, positive functions for the problem behaviour in different circumstances. The teacher asks the student who is frequently out of seat to confine the problem behaviour to the end of the lesson when the student could help to collect books and equipment.

Ecosystemic evaluation

Ecosystemic evaluation requires a comparison between pre-intervention baselines and the end points of interventions with respect to either increases in positive interactions or decreases in negative interactions. This type of evaluation will need to encompass, i.e. identify, the various systems and their interactions. For example:

- positive and negative interactions between students, students and teachers, parents and teachers may need to be evaluated;

- changes in perceptions and interpretations need to be identified and evaluated.

Behavioural, cognitive and sociometric assessment techniques and forms can be used to evaluate changes in interactions and perceptions of those involved in the interventions. Observable changes in interactions can be recorded through the use of observation schedules. Changes in perceptions and interpretations can be elicited through questionnaires, rating scales and checklists.

The aim of an ecosystemic evaluation is to see whether the use of an intervention, e.g. reframing, has brought about a new cycle of positive interactions. Given that behaviour problems are seen as arising through negative interactions then evaluation should aim to establish that all the changes in the contributory systems have been evaluated.

8 The ecological perspective

The ecological model

The ecological or social ecological model looks upon an institution as a system or organisation embedded within a specific context. Kurt Lewin (1935) maintained that events could not be considered in isolation from their context. Behaviour is a function of person–environment interactions. Explanations of the functioning of a system or organisation are concerned with the functions of the system as a whole and its subsystems. Systems are envisaged as *multi-level* and *multi-factorial*, that is there are different levels of analysis and different factors to be considered when describing any given system. Institutions are perceived as having a number of functions that can be evaluated.

Environmental perceptions and subjective responses play a significant role in this model. Identical systems and environments can be perceived differently depending on attitudes and expectations. People evaluate environments differently depending on their perceptions and feelings.

The school can be analysed as a system with component subsystems. It can also be looked upon as a multi-level system: the classroom, the pastoral system, the management system and the school as a whole. The school system is also multi-factorial in that many factors influence the school system and subsystems. Particular emphasis is placed on the social networks and physical/spatial environment in the school. The ethos or social climate of the school is seen as having an independent influence on the school as a system.

Behaviour is seen holistically, i.e. as being influenced by the social and physical environment. Individual behaviour is seen as embedded in a specific social and physical context. Personal space (Katz, 1937) is another ecological concept that describes people's attitudes towards the space surrounding their bodies. Problem behaviours can arise when others are perceived as intruding into or invading those spaces. Problem behaviour is influenced or even generated by ecological factors in specific contexts. The management structure, the pastoral system, the school ethos all act synergistically to influence individual behaviour.

Beyond the school context other systems can be considered as influencing the problem behaviour. Bronfenbrenner's (1992) *ecological systems model* represents embedded systems that have a reciprocal influence on each other. There are microsystems that comprise roles and relationships (e.g. peer groups), mesosystems (e.g. schools' relationships with parents), exosystems (e.g. parents' relationships with other parents) and macrosystems which comprise all types of systems within a cultural context. Systems influence problem behaviour and problem behaviour influences systems.

The ecological approach to behaviour

The ecological approach looks at the physical-spatial and social environments and their influence on behaviour.

The spatial environment refers, for example, to the amount of space, spatial density, location, the level of crowding experienced, split-sites and open plan buildings. Locations are seen as having particular significance, i.e. the influence of particular people and objects in the immediate surroundings of students (the *molar ecological environment*, Barker, 1968). Students' perceptions of their use of space and the use of space by others are considered to be significant in influencing behaviour. The physical and biological environment refers to such factors as temperature, light and noise. All these factors are seen as possible influences on behaviour in the school as a whole and in classrooms.

The organisational environment refers to factors such as school and class size, school structure, school ethos and classroom environment. Interactions between teachers and students and between students also influence behaviour in classrooms and the school as a whole. Moos's (1979) *social-ecological approach* focuses on person–environment interactions and their reciprocal influences. These interactions are mediated through selection, cognitive appraisal, motivation, adaptation and coping. Through the influence of these factors students may experience alienation, low self-esteem and academic failure.

Evaluation of the ecological perspective

The ecological perspective focuses on the influence of systems and subsystems on behaviour. It also emphasises the influence of the physical, spatial and social environments on behaviour. Problem behaviour is not seen in isolation from systems or the environment. Systemic factors have effects on groups as well as individuals. Problem behaviour is inevitably contextual, varying across different contexts and also between different systems. Problem behaviours may arise in some subjects, with some teachers but not others. Personal variables are seen as interacting reciprocally with environmental variables in producing and influencing problem behaviour. Ecological intervention focuses on systemic change as well as individual change and regards both as inextricably linked.

Ecological assessment

Primarily, ecological assessment focuses on whole-school management of learning and behaviour, on the school ethos, on teacher expectations, on perceptions of the classroom environment and on student evaluations of their school and peer relationships.

Whole-school behaviour management needs to be expressed in the form of a whole-school behaviour policy. A behaviour policy should start from a baseline assessment of the incidence and prevalence of different types of behaviour in the school as a whole, i.e. in public spaces as well as classrooms.

Teacher and student perceptions and expectations of the school and classroom environment can be collected and collated through self-report surveys to provide a baseline. Teacher–student and student–student interactions can be assessed through student shadowing exercises across different contexts, on different days and at different times. Variations in behaviour may become apparent and indicate the influence of social and environmental factors, e.g. the effects of streaming, teaching styles, teaching pedagogy, seating and grouping arrangements on behaviour.

Moos's *Classroom Environment Scale* lists a number of factors to be considered when assessing a classroom environment, e.g. the level of student involvement, the level of affiliation with other students and classroom rules. Lee *et al.* (1983) include other factors, e.g. participation in decision-making, responsiveness to student needs, liked, just and safe environments. In some cases *trace measures* may be used, e.g. accretion measures of the amount of graffiti and litter in a given area. These measures can be used to provide some indication of students' attitudes towards school.

Ecological formulation

An ecological formulation sees behaviour as being influenced by different types of systemic or environmental factors, i.e. physical, spatial, social and organisational factors operating in a specific context.

Problem behaviour is seen primarily as the result of person–environment interaction. Personal variables (e.g. temperament and a cognitive deficit) interact with environmental variables (e.g. seating arrangements) in a specific context (a French lesson) to produce problem behaviour. For example a student with a quick temper and reading difficulties, sitting next to a similar student in French, starts a fight over seats.

An ecological formulation therefore considers a range of ecological or systemic factors and describes how they could be influencing the problem behaviour, but also how the problem behaviour could be influencing systems.

Ecological intervention

Ecological interventions aim at bringing about positive changes in specific systems that will enable negative behaviours to be replaced by positive behaviours. The following types of interventions may be tried depending on the problem behaviour:

- changing peer group dynamics through seating and group plans or through changes in classes or forms;

- restructuring forms or classes which may positively change the dynamics of a year group;

- changing teachers' and students' negative perceptions and expectations of each other;

- changing teaching styles, e.g. from authoritarian to authoritative or from *deviance-amplification* to *deviance-insulative strategies* (Hargreaves, 1975);

- increasing participation in classroom and school decision-making, e.g. class and school councils;

- changing classroom organisation, e.g. distribution of materials and equipment and the physical layout of the classroom to minimise disruption;

- changing elements of the pastoral system, e.g. pastoral roles and referral processes;

- changing the school ethos, e.g. implementing effective whole-school policies related to learning as well as behaviour;

- changing home–school relationships, e.g. implementing home–school agreements.

Interventions should be directed at those systems that are seen as directly or indirectly influencing particular problem behaviours.

Ecological evaluation

Ecological evaluation assesses the effects of ecological interventions on problem behaviour. This involves establishing a pre-intervention baseline and assessing changes in behaviour when ecological variables are altered. Changes in the physical, spatial and social ecologies of classrooms and schools may affect the behaviour of groups as well as individuals. The effects of some ecological interventions are more easily evaluated than are others, e.g. changes in seating arrangements and grouping of students. A change in seating plan may positively affect the group dynamics in classrooms. Restructuring of forms or classes may positively affect the dynamics of a year group.

The effects of interventions on student perceptions, attitudes and expectations also need to be evaluated. The social and physical environments could remain unchanged but students' perceptions may change positively towards those environments leading to a decrease in problem behaviour. With regard to teachers' perceptions of their students' school adjustment this may depend on the teachers' application of personal criteria. Teachers' evaluation of problem behaviour may vary significantly depending on their perceptions. Teachers may perceive the same student differently to the extent that the student is problematic for some and not others. Students frequently relate differently to different teachers and different contexts. Where this occurs evaluation should tease out these variations as they may have implications for future interventions.

Bibliography

Alberto, P.A. and Troutman, A.C. (1990) *Applied Behavior Analysis for Teachers*, 3rd edn,. Columbus, Ohio: Merrill.

Alloy, L. *et al.* (1999) *Abnormal Psychology: Current Perspectives*, 8th edn. London: McGraw-Hill.

Ayers, H. *et al.* (1996) *Assessing Individual Needs: A Practical Approach*, 2nd edn. London: David Fulton Publishers.

Bandura, A. (1977) *Social Learning Theory*. Englewood Cliffs, NJ: Prentice-Hall.

Bandura, A. (1997) *Self-efficacy: The Exercise of Control*. New York: Freeman.

Barker, R.G. (1968) *Ecological Psychology: Concepts and Methods for Studying the Environment of Human Behaviour*. Stanford, CA: Stanford University Press.

Barrett, M. and Trevitt, J. (1991) *Attachment Behaviour and the Schoolchild*. London: Tavistock/Routledge.

Bateman, A. and Holmes, J. (1995) *Introduction to Psychoanalysis*. London: Routledge.

Beck, A.T. (1989) *Cognitive Therapy and the Emotional Disorders*. London: Penguin.

Bertalanffy, L. von (1968) *General Systems Theory: Foundation, Development, Applications*. New York: Braziller.

Bettelheim, B. (1991) *The Uses of Enchantment*. Harmondsworth: Penguin.

Bliss, T. and Robinson, G. (1995) *Developing Circle Time*. Lucky Duck.

Bowlby, J. (1978) *Attachment and Loss*, Vols 1–3. Harmondsworth: Penguin Education.

Bowlby, J. (1979) *The Making and Breaking of Affectional Bonds*. London: Routledge.

Bronfenbrenner, U. (1979) *The Ecology of Human Development*. Cambridge, MA: Harvard University Press.

Bronfenbrenner, U. (1992) 'Ecological systems theory', in R. Vasta (ed.) *Six Theories of Child Development*. London: Jessica Kingsley.

Brown, D. and Pedder, J. (1979) *Introduction to Psychotherapy*. London: Routledge.

Brunas-Wagstaff, J. (1998) *Personality: A Cognitive Approach*. London: Routledge.

Carr, A. (1999) *The Handbook of Child and Adolescent Psychology: A Contextual Approach*. London: Routledge.

Caspari, I. (1976) *Troublesome Children in the Classroom*. London: Routledge.

Cave, S. (1998) *Applying Psychology to the Environment*. London: Hodder & Stoughton.

Cave, S. (1999) *Therapeutic Approaches in Psychology*. London: Routledge.

Clarke, D. and Murray, M. (eds) (1996) *Developing Behaviour Policies*. London: David Fulton Publishers.

Clarke, S. (1998) *Targeting Assessment in the Primary Classroom*. London: Hodder & Stoughton Educational.

Cooper, P. (1993) *Effective Schools for Disaffected Students: Integration and Segregation*. London: Routledge.

Cooper, P. *et al.* (1994) *Emotional and Behavioural Difficulties: Theory to Practice*. London: Routledge.

Coopersmith, S. (1967) *The Antecedents of Self-esteem*. San Francisco: Freeman.

Covey, S. R. (1992) *The Seven Habits of Highly Effective People*. London: Simon & Shuster.

Craighead, L.W. *et al.* (1994) *Cognitive and Behavioral Interventions*. Needham Heights, MA: Allyn & Bacon.

Cramer, D. (1992) *Personality and Psychotherapy: Theory, Practice and Research*. Milton Keynes: Open University Press.

Daniels, H. and Corfie, L. (1993) 'The management of discipline in special schools', in V. Varma (ed.) *The Management of Behaviour in Schools*. Harlow: Longman.

DfE (1994) *Pupils with Problems*. HMSO.

Dobson, K.S. (ed.) (1988) *Handbook of Cognitive-Behavioural Therapies*. London: Hutchinson.

Dobson, K.S. and Craig, K.D. (1996) *Advances in Cognitive-Behavioral Therapy*. Thousand Oaks, CA: SAGE Publications.

Dowling, E. and Osborne, E. (eds) (1994) *The Family and the School: A Joint Systems Approach to Problems with Children*, 2nd edn. London: Routledge.

Dreikurs, R. (1982) *Maintaining Sanity in the Classroom*. London: HarperCollins.

Durrant, M. (1995) *Creative Strategies for School Problems*. London: WW Norton.

D'Zurilla, T.J. (1986) *Problem-Solving Therapy*. New York: Springer.

Ellis, A. (1962) *Reason and Emotion in Psychotherapy*. New York: Lyle Stuart.

Emerson, E. (1995) *Challenging Behaviour*. Cambridge: Cambridge University Press.

Epanchin, B. and Paul, J. (1987) *Emotional Problems of Childhood and Adolescence: A Multidisciplinary Perspective*. Oxford: Maxwell Macmillan.

Eysenck, M.J. (1994) *Perspectives on Psychology*. Hove: Lawrence Erlbaum Associates.

Faber, A. and Mazlish, E. (1980) *How to Talk So Kids Will Listen and How to Listen So Kids Will Talk*. New York: Avon Books.

Faraone, S.V. *et al.* (1999) *Genetics of Mental Disorders*. New York: The Guilford Press.

Feindler, E. and Ecton, R. (1986) *Adolescent Anger Control: Cognitive-Behavioral Techniques*. Oxford: Pergamon.

Fontana, D. (1981) *Psychology for Teachers*. Basingstoke: BPS Books, Macmillan.

Fontana, D. (1993) *Psychology for Teachers*, 2nd edn. Basingstoke: BPS Books, Macmillan.

Freud, A. (1966) *Normality and Pathology in Childhood*. London: Karnac.

Freud, A. (1986) *The Ego and the Mechanisms of Defence*. London: Hogarth.

Freud, S. (1984) *The Theory of Psychoanalysis*. Harmondsworth: Penguin.

Galvin, P. (1999) *Behaviour and Discipline in Schools*, Vol. 2. London: David Fulton Publishers.

Goldenberg, I. and Goldenberg, H. (1996) *Family Therapy: An Overview*, 4th edn. Pacific Grove, CA: Brooks/Cole Publishing.

Goldthorpe, M. (1998) *Effective IEPs Through Circletime*. Learning Development Aids.

Goleman, D. (1996) *Emotional Intelligence*. London: Bloomsbury.

Graham, P. (ed.) (1998) *Cognitive-Behaviour Therapy for Children and Families*. Cambridge: Cambridge University Press.

Greenhalgh, P. (1994) *Emotional Growth and Learning*. London: Routledge.

Haley, J. (1970) 'Family therapy', *International Journal of Psychiatry*, 9.

Hanko, G. (1991) *Special Needs in Ordinary Classrooms*. Oxford: Blackwell.

Hargreaves, D.H. (1975) *Interpersonal Relations and Education*. London: Routledge & Kegan Paul.

Hastings, N. and Schwieso, J. (1987) *New Directions in Educational Psychology: 2. Behaviour and Motivation in the Classroom*. London: Falmer Press.

Hawton, K. *et al.* (eds) (1989) *Cognitive Behaviour Therapy for Psychiatric Problems: A Practical Guide.* Oxford: Oxford University Press.

Herbert, M. (1981) *Behavioural Treatment of Children with Problems: A Practice Manual*, 2nd edn. London: Harcourt Brace Jovanovitch College Publishers.

Herbert, M. (1988) *Working with Children and their Families.* London: The British Psychological Society in association with Routledge.

Herbert, M. (1991) *Clinical Child Psychology: Social Learning, Development and Behaviour.* Chichester: Wiley.

Jones, R.A. (1995) *The Child–School Interface: Environment and Behaviour.* London: Cassell.

Juvonen, J. and Wentzel, K.R. (eds) (1996) *Social Motivation: Understanding Children's School Adjustment.* Cambridge: Cambridge University Press.

Katz, P. (1937) *Animals and Men.* New York: Longmans, Green.

Kazdin, A. (1988) *Child Psychotherapy: Developing and Identifying Effective Treatments.* London: Routledge.

Kazdin, A. (1994) *Behavior Modification in Applied Settings.* Pacific Grove: Brooks/Cole.

Kelly, G.A. (1955) *The Psychology of Personal Constructs*, Vols 1 and 2. New York: Norton.

Kendall, P.C. and Braswell, L. (1993) *Cognitive-Behavioral Therapy for Impulsive Children*, 2nd edn. London: Guilford Press.

Klein, M. (1988) *Envy and Gratitude and Other Works 1946–63.* London: Virago.

Kline, P. (1993) *Personality: The Psychometric View.* London: Routledge.

Lader, M. and Herrington, R. (1990) *Biological Treatments in Psychiatry.* Oxford: Oxford University Press.

Lawrence, D. (1987) *Enhancing Self-esteem in the Classroom.* London: PCP.

Lee, P.C. *et al.* (1983) 'Elementary school children's perceptions of their actual and ideal school experience: a developmental study', *Journal of Educational Psychology*, 75.

Lewin, K.A. (1935) *A Dynamic Theory of Personality: Selected Papers.* New York: McGraw-Hill.

Long, R. and Fogell, D. (1999) *Supporting Pupils with Emotional Difficulties.* London: David Fulton Publishers.

McGrath, M. (1999) *The Art of Teaching Peacefully.* London: David Fulton Publishers.

McLeod, J. (1993) *An Introduction to Counselling.* Buckingham: Open University Press.

Maslow, A. (1998) *Towards a Psychology of Being.* Chichester: John Wiley & Sons.

Meichenbaum, D. (1977) *Cognitive-Behavior Modification.* New York: Plenum.

Meichenbaum, D.H. and Cameron, R. (1973) 'Training schizophrenics to talk to themselves: a means of developing attributional controls', *Behavior Therapy*, 4.

Meichenbaum, D.H. and Goodman, J. (1971) 'Training impulsive children to talk to themselves: a means of developing self-control', *Journal of Abnormal Psychology*, 77.

Mental Health Foundation (1999) *Bright Futures: Promoting Children and Young People's Mental Health.* Mental Health Foundation.

Messer, D. and Miller, S. (eds) (1999) *Exploring Developmental Psychology.* London: Arnold.

Minuchin, S. (1974) *Families and Family Therapy.* Cambridge, MA: Harvard University Press.

Mischel, W. (1973) 'Towards a cognitive social learning reconceptualization of personality', *Psychological Review*, 80.

Molnar, A. and Lindquist, B. (1989) *Changing Problem Behaviour in Schools.* San Francisco: Jossey-Bass.

Monte, C.F. (1999) *Beneath the Mask: An Introduction to Theories of Personality*, 6th edn. New York: Harcourt Brace.

Moos, R.H. (1979) *Evaluating Educational Environments*. San Francisco: Jossey-Bass.

Mortimore, P. *et al.* (1988) *School Matters: The Junior Years*. Somerset: Open Books.

Moseley, J. (1993) *Turn Your School Round*, LDA.

Nicolson, D. and Ayers, H. (1995) *Individual Counselling: Theory and Practice*. London: David Fulton Publishers.

Nicolson, D. and Ayers, H. (1997) *Adolescent Problems: A Practical Guide for Parents and Teachers*. London: David Fulton Publishers.

Nolte, D.L. and Harris, R. (1998) *Children Learn What They Live*. New York: Workman Publishing. The poem can also be found at www.empowermentresources.com

Norwich, B. (1990) *Reappraising Special Needs Education*. London: Cassell.

O'Brien, T. (1998) *Promoting Positive Behaviour*. London: David Fulton Publishers.

Premack, D. (1965) 'Reinforcement theory', in D. Levine (ed.) *Nebraska Symposium on Motivation* (Vol. 13). Lincoln: University of Nebraska Press.

Robertson, J. (1989) *Effective Classroom Control*, 2nd edn. London: Hodder & Stoughton.

Rogers, B. (1990a) *The Language of Discipline*. Plymouth: Northcote House.

Rogers, B. (1990b) *Supporting Teachers in the Workplace*. Queensland: Jacaranda Press.

Rogers, B. (1990c) *You Know the Fair Rule*. Harlow: Longman.

Rogers, B. (1994) *Behaviour Recovery*. Melbourne: ACER.

Rogers, C. (1974) *On Becoming a Person*, London: Constable.

Ronen, T. (1997) *Cognitive Developmental Therapy with Children*. Chichester: Wiley & Sons.

Rosenbaum M. (1990) 'The role of learned resourcefulness in self-control of health behaviour', in M. Rosenbaum (ed.) *Learned Resourcefulness: On Coping Skills, Self-control and Adaptive Behaviour*. New York: Springer.

Rosenbaum, M. (1993) 'The three functions of self-control behaviour: redressive, reformative and experiential', *Journal of Work and Stress*.

Rotter, J.B. (1966) 'Generalised expectancies for internal versus external control of reinforcement', *Psychological Monographs*, 80.

Rutter, M. *et al.* (1979) *Fifteen Thousand Hours: Secondary Schools and Their Effects on Children*. London: Open Books.

Rycroft, Charles (1968) *A Critical Dictionary of Psychoanalysis*. Harmondsworth: Penguin.

Salzberger-Wittenberg, I. (1970) *Psycho-Analytic Insight and Relationships: A Kleinian Approach*. London: Routledge.

Salzberger-Wittenberg, I. (1993) *The Emotional Experience of Teaching and Learning*. London: Routledge.

Schopler, E. (1997) 'Implementation of TEACCH philosophy', in D.J. Cohen and F.R. Volkmar (eds) *Handbook of Autism and Pervasive Developmental Disorders*, 2nd edn. New York: Wiley.

Selvini-Palazzoli *et al.* (1974) 'The treatment of children through brief therapy of their parents', *Family Process*, 13.

Sheldon, B. (1995) *Cognitive-Behavioural Therapy*. London: Routledge.

Silber, K. (1999) *The Physiological Basis of Behaviour*. London: Routledge.

Skinner, B.F. (1993) *About Behaviorism*. London: Penguin.

Smith, A. (1996) *Accelerated Learning in the Classroom*. Network Educational Press.

Spiegler, M.D. and Guevrement, D.C. (1998) *Contemporary Behavior Therapy*, 3rd edn. Pacific Grove: Brooks/Cole.

Street, E. and Dryden, W. (eds) (1988) *Family Therapy in Britain*. Milton Keynes: Open University Press.

Trower, P. *et al.* (1988) *Cognitive-Behavioural Counselling in Action*. London: SAGE Publications.

Vygotsky, V. (1962) *Thought and Language*. Cambridge, MA: MIT Press.

Walker, J.E. and Shea, T.M. (1991) *Behavior Management*. Maxwell Macmillan International Editions.

Wenar, C. (1994) *Developmental Psychopathology: From Infancy through Adolescence*, 3rd edn. London: McGraw Hill.

Wheldall, K. *et al.* (1986) *Behavioural Analysis in Educational Psychology*. Beckenham: Croom Helm.

Wing, L. (1993) 'The definition and prevalence of autism: a review', *European Child and Adolescent Psychiatry*, 2.

Winnicott, D. (1971) *Playing and Reality*. London: Tavistock/Routledge.

Winnicott, D. (1991) *The Child, the Family and the Outside World*. Harmondsworth. Penguin.

Wipfler, P. (1990) *Listening to Children*. Palo Alto: Parents Leadership Institute.

Wipfler, P. (1995a) *Setting Limits With Children*. Palo Alto: Parents Leadership Institute.

Wipfler, P. (1995b) *Supporting Adolescents*. Palo Alto: Parents Leadership Institute.

Woolf, R. and Dryden, W. (1996) *Handbook of Counselling Psychology*. London: Sage.

Videos

Bliss, T. and Robinson, G. *Developing Circle Time*. Lucky Duck.

Moseley, J. *The Whole School Quality Circle Time Model*. Jenny Moseley.

Resources

COGNITIVE ASSESSMENT PUPIL QUESTIONNAIRE

This form can be used as a means of assessing a pupil's thoughts, attitudes, expectations and beliefs in the school context.
Circle appropriate number on each continuum and <u>underline</u> or add relevant words
Unless otherwise indicated: 1 = Poor   3 = OK   5 = Excellent

BEHAVIOUR:

What do you THINK about your behaviour in:

1) Classrooms *1 2 3 4 5*		2) Corridors	*1 2 3 4 5*	
3) Assembly *1 2 3 4 5*		4) Toilets	*1 2 3 4 5*	
5) Playground *1 2 3 4 5*		6) Outside school *1 2 3 4 5*		

7) How do you generally behave?   *1 2 3 4 5*

Interfering Helpful Unhelpful Rude Polite Violent Friendly Talkative Loud Quiet Hardworking Lazy

8) What do you THINK about changing your behaviour?

1	*2*	*3*	*4*	*5*
Unable to change		May be able to change		Able to change

I don't have the power   I do have the power   I don't want to   I want to
Teachers stop me   Teachers will help me   Pupils stop me   Other pupils will help me

9) What do you think of yourself?   *1 2 3 4 5*

Confident Lacking in confidence Attractive Unattractive Clever Stupid Interested Disinterested

10) In general, do you THINK teachers' behaviour towards you is:
                              1 2 3 4 5

Helpful Unhelpful Unfriendly Polite Rude Friendly Caring Aggressive Interested Not interested
In particular?

11) What do you THINK about the behaviour of other pupils towards:

YOURSELF:	*EACH OTHER:*	*TEACHERS:*
1 2 3 4 5	*1 2 3 4 5*	*1 2 3 4 5*

12) What do you think of your school? *1 2 3 4 5*

Too small	*Just the right size*	*Too big*	*Poorly decorated*	*Pleasantly decorated*
Badly designed	*Too hot*	*Too cold*	*Badly lit*	*Too noisy* *Too crowded*

WORK:

---

13) What do you THINK about the level of work?

1 = Too difficult   *2 = Difficult*   *3 = Just right*   *4 = Easy*   *5 = Too easy*

Mathematics	1 2 3 4 5		1 2 3 4 5
English	1 2 3 4 5		1 2 3 4 5
Science	1 2 3 4 5		1 2 3 4 5

---

14) What do you THINK about the relevance of the work to you?

1 = None   *2 = Little*   *3 = Some*   *4 = A lot*   *5 = Completely*

Mathematics	1 2 3 4 5		1 2 3 4 5
English	1 2 3 4 5		1 2 3 4 5
Science	1 2 3 4 5		1 2 3 4 5

---

15) What do you THINK about the level of achievement?

1 = Poor   *2 = Not very good*   *3 = Average*   *4 = Good*   *5 = Very good*

Mathematics	1 2 3 4 5		1 2 3 4 5
English	1 2 3 4 5		1 2 3 4 5
Science	1 2 3 4 5		1 2 3 4 5

---

16) Do you THINK you can do better?

1 = Not at all   *2 = Possibly*   *3 = Some*   *4 = Quite a lot*   *5 = A lot*

Mathematics	1 2 3 4 5		1 2 3 4 5
English	1 2 3 4 5		1 2 3 4 5
Science	1 2 3 4 5		1 2 3 4 5

---

17) What do you THINK about your effort?

1 = Poor   *2 = Not very good*   *3 = Average*   *4 = Good*   *5 = Very good*

Mathematics	1 2 3 4 5		1 2 3 4 5
English	1 2 3 4 5		1 2 3 4 5
Science	1 2 3 4 5		1 2 3 4 5

Any other comments?

INTERVIEW SHEET for CARERS

Name: [   ]   **Age:** [   ]   **Date:** [   ][   ][   ]

School: [   ]   **Form/Class:** [   ]

This sheet is intended as a structure for interviewing carers about their thoughts and feelings with respect to the pupil

1) Are they a problem to you?

Never   Occasionally   Sometimes   A lot

2) Where are they a problem?

At home   In other people's homes   In the street

In shops   In the park   Public places   Other

3) What kind of problem(s)?

1 = Rarely   2 = Occasionally   3 = Regularly

Attention-seeking	1 2 3		Bullying	1 2 3	
Disobedient	1 2 3		Temper outburst	1 2 3	
Depressed	1 2 3		Wetting/soiling	1 2 3	
Verbally aggressive	1 2 3		Staying out late	1 2 3	
Physically aggressive	1 2 3		Noisy	1 2 3	
Argumentative	1 2 3		Other	1 2 3	

4) What seems to lead to the problem(s)?

When asked to do something by an adult/child

When they want something material e.g. clothes or non-material e.g. attention

When someone comes to the home – an adult/child

When they are with their peer group

When limits/rules are imposed

Other

5) What do you do about the problem(s)?

Tell them off   Nothing in particular

Discuss the problem with them   Don't know what to do

Punish them   Other

Bribe them

Encourage them to do better

6) What punishments do you use?

How effective are they?

7) What rewards or encouragements do you use?

How effective are they?

8) In what ways would you like your child to change?

Quieter	More helpful
More obedient	Work harder at school
Friendlier	Be more respectful
More polite	Happier
More considerate	More relaxed
Other	

9) Do you expect your child to change?

YES/POSSIBLY/NO

What might make it difficult?

Character or temperament	Lack of communication skills
Lack of social skills	Poor learning skills
Bad influence of friends/peers	Acts without thinking
Rejects help	Don't know what to do
Other	Teachers/school pick on him/her

10) What are your general feelings about your child's problem(s)

Anger	Sadness
Puzzlement	Hopelessness
Discouragement	Frustration
Powerlessness	Irritation
Other	

ANALYSIS OF INTERACTIONS SHEET

Name: **Age:**   **Date:**

Form/Class: **NC Year:**

1) Describe how you perceive the interactions between yourself and the target pupil
in positive as well as negative terms

2) Describe how other staff perceive the target pupil
in positive as well as negative terms

3) Describe how you perceive the interactions between the target pupil and other pupils
in positive as well as negative terms

4) Describe how you perceive the interactions within the target pupil's family and between the family and the school

5) Describe any comparisons you are able to make between any observations undertaken of the target pupil: does this comparison highlight discrepancies or agreements? If so, what implications does it have for your picture of the pupil?

6) From the above information, summarise your perceptions and those of others and state your expectations of the target pupil.

7) If possible, REFRAME those perceptions in such a way that the target pupil's problem is redefined more positively. Describe your 'reframing'.

PUPIL SELF-CONTROL MONITORING FORM

Name: _____ **Date:** [___][___][___]

Form/Class: _____

Underline appropriate words or phrases and add any others that seem relevant

1) Where did the incident take place?

Class	Toilets	Corridor
Playground	Trip	Stairs
Dining Hall	To or from school	Gym
Assembly	Other	

2) What took place?

A pupil teased me	A teacher told me off	A pupil cussed me
A pupil took my things	A pupil annoyed me	A pupil hit me
I did something wrong	Other	

3) Who was involved?

A friend	Another pupil	An adult
Other		

4) What did you do?

Hit back	Told a teacher	Ran away
Told another adult	Shouted	Walked away calmly
Cried	Talked it through	Lost my temper
Broke something	Told a friend	Took no notice
Other		

5) How did you feel?

I felt . . .   I felt like . . .

6) How upset did you get?

Extremely   Very   Mildly   A little   Not at all

7) How well did you control yourself?

Extremely   Very   Mildly   A little   Not at all

8) What could you do differently next time?

PRIMARY COGNITIVE PUPIL QUESTIONNAIRE

This form can be used as a means of assessing a pupil's thoughts, attitudes, expectations and beliefs in the school context.

Circle appropriate number on each continuum and <u>underline</u> or add relevant words

Unless otherwise indicated: 1 = Poor   3 = OK   5 = Excellent

BEHAVIOUR:

What do you THINK about your behaviour in:		
1) Classrooms *1 2 3 4 5*	2) Corridors	*1 2 3 4 5*
3) Assembly *1 2 3 4 5*	4) Toilets	*1 2 3 4 5*
5) Playground *1 2 3 4 5*	6) Outside school *1 2 3 4 5*	

7) How do you generally behave?   *1   2   3   4   5*

Interfering Helpful Unhelpful Rude Polite Violent Friendly Talkative Loud Quiet Hardworking Lazy

8) What do you THINK about the behaviour of other pupils towards:

YOURSELF:	*EACH OTHER:*	*TEACHERS:*
1 2 3 4 5	*1 2 3 4 5*	*1 2 3 4 5*

9) What do you like about school/like doing at school?

10) What don't you like about school/don't like doing at school?

11) What do you do well at school/not do well at school?

12) Which pupils do you like to play with/work with?

Index

106